# ANNA HARVEY

# TIMELESS STYLE

Dressing Well for the Rest of your Life

Published by Double-Barrelled Books
Double-Barrelled Books
www.double-barrelled-books.com

Editor
Sian Parkhouse

Design
Alfonso Iacurci and Helen McFarland
Cultureshock Media

Production Manager
Nicola Vanstone

Printed By
Toppan Leefung Printing Ltd.
www.toppanleefung.com

Design and layouts © 2016
Double-Barrelled Books 2016

Text and illustrations © 2016 Anna Harvey

A CIP catalogue record for this book is
available from the British Library
ISBN: 978-0-9571500-96

# Contents

# Foreword

My fashion career, which has spanned many years, has been spent in the publishing world, mainly on Vogue magazine. Over that time I have been asked many, many times for advice about what-to-wear to various events.

As a result, and as I grow older and certainly fashion-wiser myself, I have decided to try and set down some helpful guide lines for those who feel they need it – and *Timeless Style: Dressing Well for the Rest of your Life* – is the happy result. I hope you may enjoy it and find it useful in helping to make decisions about what may or may not suit your figure type; what items to spend money on and where; what to look for on the high street; and what to wear to some of the events you may have to attend.

This is very much a book of general advice, because women come in all shapes and sizes and it would be well nigh impossible to solve all the questions you may have. But I have tried to address the most common queries I have received over the years and although of course I don't believe I have all the answers I hope you will find some of the advice helpful.

As we and our figures change, many of us need that guidance at times. There are of course no rules and we may all wear what we please, but I believe the age for a mini skirt and thigh boots is well and truly over for me, and perhaps for you too, but there are many other options out there which are just as interesting and attractive, without rendering you invisible.

When I started writing this book I had many preconceptions about what I and other women should and should not wear after a certain age. In the process I have found that some of my cast-iron rules such as 'no leggings' have mellowed, and I now feel that leggings, for example, are not the pariah clothing that I believed them to be – there is a way and time for wearing them that is perfectly smart and acceptable (see pages 42–43). The same applies to sleeveless dresses and plunging décolletés – if you have the figure to carry these off, I am very envious and not at all against the idea. It is important to remain open-minded on all things sartorial, I have found, as what might be a rule for one does not necessarily apply to another. The important thing is to know when to phase out certain wardrobe favourites, as well as phasing in some pieces that may become new favourites, and I hope that here I may be able to help.

I have not only included my thoughts on what you may feel comfortable in, but also practical advice on what may suit your shape height and personality; no-one wants to hear that stage whisper 'mutton' – heaven forbid!

What I do know is that when one sees a woman looking elegant, attractive and comfortable, whatever her shape, it is a pleasure. To achieve this is not that difficult, and I very much hope that this book will help.

*AH*

# Introduction

After a certain age, fashion doesn't matter – it's style that counts, and that is eminently achievable, and not difficult; it's fun to look as good as possible, expressing yourself through your clothes.

It is important to beware of becoming too set in your ways. In the same way that it is all too easy to get in the way of thinking that you never drink Earl Grey or hate musicals (for example!), only to miraculously discover that you don't think that way at all, one can also build up a set of self-rules about clothes that actually you haven't taken out and shaken down for years – I can't wear trousers/ skirts; I never wear blue, and so on. But if you are not tied by fashion – oh what a relief – you can look at all your self-imposed rules and start a new stylish life.

Key to the process is not to think in terms of age – if you think you are dressing for your age, there is every chance that you will simply dress in a way that is frumpy and just too old. There are really no age-appropriate clothes, there are just clothes that make you feel and look good – and there are also things that really no longer look good, like short frilly skirts or too-cropped tops. The easiest way to look older is to dress 'younger'. Just don't do it. If you're asking yourself, 'does this make me look younger' you're in the wrong place.

So now read on...

# How to Dress

Think of this chapter as being the one that you find early on in every diet book; the one which tells you to take a hard look at your eating habits, to throw out the unhealthy food and take stock of how you want to be–the only difference is that in this book we are talking about how to dress well, rather than how to eat well.

But of course there are similarities between getting yourself physically in shape and getting your wardrobe in shape, for indeed the long-term goals are the same – to look good and feel better and more confident about yourself.

There are also similarities between the two ideas, in that we suggest how to look at yourself in a different way – to take stock of your body shape as well as your wardrobe and make a plan for the future that is based on sensible ideas with a bit of inspiration thrown in. And once you've looked properly at your body, wobbles and all, then we show you what shapes and styles to look for, both in your existing wardrobe and when you are looking for something new.

# First things First: Analysing your Shape

It is true to say – we all do it – that, after a certain age, most women simply don't see, or don't want to see, what they look like. So rule one is to become familiar with the way your body is at the moment, and accept what you see.

For example, when you go clothes shopping, make the most of shop changing rooms, and when you are in them, stripped off, use the mirrors – all of them! Look at yourself from the front, of course, but also, and more importantly, view yourself from the side and from the back. That's where you see the unpalatable truths – the floppy bits, the tummy and thigh bulges, the things that people may notice when you walk into a room. And check out the back view – under-arm and bra bulges, a stoop of the shoulders and, of course, the bottom! Test out your posture, too, and notice how much better you look when your shoulders are not sloped and your back is straight.

'The older body arrives gradually so you can evolve slowly with no sudden changes.' — Grace Coddington

# Changing Shape as you Age

We all change shape as we age – and although that does not necessarily mean getting larger, many of us do just that, particularly round the middle. There is definitely a psychological barrier to accepting that you might be a size larger than you used to be, that you are bigger than you want, to be, or even that simply because you can just about squeeze into your usual size, you still look good in it – I'm always thinking that I am a size smaller than I really am.

'When I was younger I wore longer shirts, but I have lost height over the years and really big shirts swamp me so I wear them shorter now.' — Grace Coddington

Of course some labels – usually the more expensive – are cut more generously than others, so your wardrobe might already contain several apparently different sizes, although they all fit you the same way.

The fact is, though, that whatever the label says, you definitely look, and just as importantly, feel, a lot slimmer if clothes are a bit looser on you – not just trousers, but almost everything; looser clothes disguise the bits you'd rather hide and soften the silhouette. So, never buy anything too tight. Rather than squeezing into a size 12, for example, perhaps you should try on a size 14? And if it makes you feel better to cut out the label, then by all means, do it. Nobody will know except you. It's just a number, after all. We have all learnt the lesson of buying shoes a size too small, and dealing with the subsequent agony...

**Waists and Tummies**

I think you've got to accept that even if you are not overweight, you may be becoming thicker around the waist and there's not much you can do about that (although exercise can help) since it is an undeniable, if unpalatable fact that our metabolism slows with age, and there is also a change in hormone levels associated with the menopause.

'The only place you never gain weight is your shoulders.' — Donna Karan

'Rather than squeezing into a size 12, for example, perhaps you should try a size 14 and if it makes you feel better to cut out the label, then by all means do – no-one will know except you.'

- As far as the tummy is concerned, by a certain age most people have lost some muscle tone – anyone who has had a child particularly – and some of the elasticity of their stomach muscles will have gone.
- I always used to hate elasticated trousers and elasticated skirts and most people would shriek at the idea, but actually they are often the only practical solution if you want to wear a straight skirt or trousers. Model Jerry Hall, however, famously said, never wear an elasticated waistline because if you do you will never know if you gaining weight or inches. She does have a point.

- Even if you hold your tummy in when you are standing, the minute you sit down, it all comes out in the front; it droops like the dough for a loaf of bread, over the top of the waistband – not a great look. I mean I could starve myself, but the last thing to look better would be the waist, so tight-waisted things are no longer any good for me.
- You do need some give somewhere – perhaps just around the back.
- The late Jean Muir designed very desirable, well-cut wool crepe skirts that had waistbands that were slightly elasticated – frumpy they were not.

'Taking the veil is a wise idea as skin wrinkles. A chiffon shawl is a way of coping with the fact that so many dresses on the racks are sleeveless.' — Suzy Menkes

## Hiding the Upper Arms

Whenever I go into a boutique or dress department, I walk around once, very fast, to see how many things hanging on the rails have sleeves. And then I pull it out to see whether it is a jacket or a dress.

If there is nothing with sleeves, I walk out again. You could ask, and I do, why don't stores always carry dresses with sleeves? And if they do stock sleeveless dresses, why don't they also stock pretty cardigans that actually go with the dresses on display? So, because they don't, I buy my cardigans separately – mostly cheap and mostly from Uniqlo, cotton in the summer, cashmere in the winter. Personally I prefer ones that button to the neck – V-neck ones are slightly more difficult to work with dress necklines; they look better worn with round necks or shirts.

**Colour and Pattern**

Before you begin to be specific about how to dress, this seems like a good place to think about colour and pattern, and their pitfalls and pleasures.

I do think that what colours you wear and what actually suits you is even more important as you get older. I really feel that as a broad rule of thumb, you have to go for softer tones of the more vibrant primary shades such as bright reds, yellows and blues. (Of course, if you're very bronzed and on the beach under a brilliant sky and golden sun you can go for any colour you like – no holds barred.) But for day-to-day life I do think that somewhat lighter, softer colours work much better with the lighter skin that seems to come as one ages.

Try not to wear too much black during the day – it is ageing; instead try grey, light or dark, or neutrals (not camel!) And not too much white or cream, other than as a T-shirt or shirt.

For some reason navy blue is seen as a difficult colour, or just another version of black. It's not of course; it is softer, warmer than black, and I think much nicer. I have worn a lot of navy over the years, particularly as an alternative to crow-like black. I find it very chic and flattering for almost any occasion, day or night. People sometimes feel that too much navy can look too like an uniform, but unless it is a severe suit – which could make you look like an airline employee – then give it a try.

Brown, too, in all its tones, is a much underrated palette – chestnut, caramel, chocolate, both milk and plain are very pretty, very flattering shades for every skin shade; even the names are enticing.

'Wear fewer white shirts as you grow older –
try colour instead, such as deep red, purple,
dark green.' — Grace Coddington

In the evening, don't ignore jewel and berry colours, which can be very flattering in evening light – sapphire, garnet, emerald; blackberry, raspberry, blueberry and damson, for example.

Black, if you really like it and can wear it, can come into its own in the evening and it is always smart. Brighten it up with jewellery, and if it is a short dress or skirt, wear sheer (as sheer as you can find) flesh-coloured tights (black sheer tights are also fine if your legs are good).

Any colour for the evening is lifted with jewellery or even a beautiful pair of shoes in a mad glamorous colour such as red, emerald, saffron or shocking pink, for example. Possibly those expensive coloured shoes you bought for that wedding might fit the bill.

Saying all that, I don't really like too many rules about colour – someone saying flatly that you can't wear yellow, for example. Do experiment – but just remember during the day, no brights, and definitely very little black. I do feel a bit of a hypocrite saying this, as I do wear black in the daytime occasionally, even in summer. This is because it was the fashion uniform during most of my career and breaking away from a habit is difficult. These days, though, when shopping, I am now definitely ditching the black and try to buy only colours and neutral shades.

'There comes a time when you have to decide what sort of woman you are and how best to interpret that successfully in how you present yourself.' — Diana Donovan

'There is no such thing as being underdressed or overdressed – just well-dressed or badly dressed.' — Charlotte Scott

# Back to Basics

It is obvious, when you think about it, that any re-think or re-working of an existing wardrobe, or indeed the planning of a wonderful new one, must begin with the right underwear. Now that you have – I hope – identified the bits of your own body that you would like hidden, improved or just generally encouraged, it is time to assess what to wear beneath what you wear.

**Bras**

It is repeated so often as to almost be a cliché, but when gravity begins to take its toll, and you can no longer rely on muscles doing the essential support work, a good bra really is an absolute necessity.

- A bra should not sit too low, but neither should it sit too high, and there should be absolutely no bulges at the back, nor at the sides beneath the armpits.
- Under wiring is not essential, but can be very helpful.
- And please, no nipples showing through a thin shirt – so always buy a bra that is moulded or lined.
- As a basic bra wardrobe, you need a dark-coloured bra – black, or maybe dark brown or grey – and a white one or, better still, one that is flesh-coloured, which looks more natural under see-through clothes...

It's a strange fact that some people seem to think that you only need one bra, which you wear until the elastic is wrinkled and the straps sagging. I even heard of someone who didn't bother to buy her own, but wore her daughters' castoffs.

# And another thing...

I really do think that it is important to have a bra fitted – or at any rate the first one that you buy from a new supplier. Personally, I don't go to a specialist bra company, but to the underwear department of any department or chain store that has professional fitters. But wherever you go, you must look at your boobs in relation to your body; it's a fact that when you get thinner – or fatter – your boobs will get larger or smaller along with the rest of your body. It's amazing how some women seem to divorce the size of their bust from their weight.

# And another thing...

It is an irony that when my friends and I were much, much younger and had quite well-proportioned, good figures, in order to keep our stomachs in check we all used to wear elasticated tubes called roll-ons, which smelled of elastic and rubber. We didn't need them then of course, but we thought we did. Then came the idea of liberation and freedom and we all gave up the bras and ditched the roll-ons. Although, in time, we went back to the bras, most of us never went back to any sort of support underwear – and still haven't, although many of us could really do with it now. It is a fact that over a certain age, support underwear is good; it makes you look better in your clothes and I think we have to learn to love it again.

## Knickers

They may be neither very attractive nor sexy but the fact is that big knickers do work, and they leave the minimum of VPL (which, as we all know, stands for Visible Panty Line). If you're like me who has a dropped bottom, that means that rather than cutting in under your bottom, which in itself doesn't look that good, the VPL can cut through bottom sag in a most unattractive way. Under full or soft skirts you can of course wear anything you like, but under a straight skirt or tight trousers you definitely do need some sort of support.

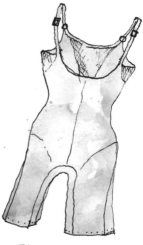

Shapewear

'If you have gained weight as you have grown older, your bosom will be bigger; a sports bra will be more comfortable.' — Grace Coddington

## Modern Support, or Shapewear as it sometimes known

The re-shaping, on a temporary basis, of the bits you don't like is big business; there are designs that smooth, firm and lift, ranging from an almost all-in-one which goes from bosom to bottom and beyond, to simple bust-shapers or sculpted briefs. Some designs are quite attractive, others more like functional armour, but the range, at every price level, means that there really is something for everyone and they do have a positive effect. Try to find pieces that – like good make-up – make you look like a better version of you, rather than a different person.

## Slips and Camisoles

If you are wearing anything vaguely sheer you must wear a slip or camisole as it unifies the look and makes the most of what you are wearing. Personally if I am out shopping for clothes I always wear a camisole or a thin vest top, as I then feel more confident trying on clothes. If you only want to buy one camisole make it flesh-coloured rather than white – and try to choose a flesh tone that is closest to your own. And for warmth in the winter you can find really fine camisole tops in knitted silk – the Swiss company Hanro makes lovely ones.

High     Unhemmed     Full plain

'No ruffles or frills. Be neat, wear a simple, stricter line. Keep the silhouette straight from the shoulder; avoid bust and waist darts and make sure the garment skims the hip. Black creates the illusion that you are slimmer on the lower half.' — Grace Coddington

# Tops

The tunic shape is the ultimate forgiving outline – I love it. You can wear it as a top or a dress – in fact if you see a tunic shape dress that you like and you are tall enough so that it stops above the knees, you can wear it over a straight skirt for a chic, up-to-date look.

- When looking at tunic tops the essential thing is that it should be neat across the shoulders and with a straight, set-in sleeve rather than a kimono-shaped sleeve, so that you look small on top with an elongated body.
- Any tunic should finish at crotch level at the very least and if you are self-conscious about your bottom or hips, look for a tunic length that will cover them and drop to thigh level.
- Tunics work in many different weights and textures: my elder daughter has a velvet tunic based loosely on an Indian kurta with side slits, and it works brilliantly in the evening with either a skirt or trousers.

Tunic top

Slim shirt

Belted shirt

# 'I love linen shirts because it doesn't matter if they are creased...'

### Shirts

I love shirts, but I am lazy about ironing so I don't own many. However, every woman should have at least one shirt in her wardrobe. I suggest at least a couple of white shirts, one in cotton and a smarter one in silk. I also love linen shirts because it doesn't matter if they are creased.

A shirt doesn't have to be fitted, it can be big – a man's shirt can work, of course, but for many of us, a woman's long shirt with pretty buttons works better because of the narrower shoulders; the shoulder width is all important in slimming the whole body.

If you feel you are slim enough, a shirt, particularly a fitted one, can look good tucked in to a belt; a tip to make the shirt hang well is that when you put it on, tuck it in tightly and then lift both arms; this will release fabric evenly around your waist giving a softer, more fluid look.

## T-Shirts

Summer basics should always include T-shirts
– several in slightly different shapes. I have
sleeveless ones, which I wear with a cotton
cardigan or a shirt over them, as well as both
short and long-sleeved ones.

- Choose non-stretchy ones, or ones with
  just a minimum of stretch; too much
  stretch has a tendency to cling to the
  lumpy bits (see overleaf).
- Always buy T-shirts at least one size larger,
  particularly if they are cheap. They will
  not cling and even after some shrinkage
  will look better than something that is
  absolutely skin tight.
- Choose white, of course, but look for other
  colours too that will work with your particular
  wardrobe. And if they are cheap –and white –
  throw them away after a season because they
  will have discoloured and have a yellow tinge.

—

Something that seems
to pass many people by
is the fact that the shape
and style of a T-shirt
actually alters slightly
every season – the
neckline alters subtly and
the shape is sometimes
more fitted, sometimes
looser, sometimes longer,
sometimes shorter, ditto
sleeve shape and length. It
is in fact incredibly ageing
to keep wearing ten-year-
old T-shirts just because
they haven't actually worn
out. Throw them out and
buy two or three new ones
– every year.

——

'Always buy T-shirts at least one size larger, particularly if they are cheap – they won't cling and will look better than something that is absolutely skin tight.'

### Elasticated

On the subject of T-shirts, those that have a certain amount of elastic in them are a mixed blessing: the added elastic does prevent cotton from bagging, but it still doesn't mean that you should buy everything tight; in fact unless the T-shirt is actually quite large on you an elastic mix can be a bit of a disaster, since a too-tight, too clingy T-shirt magnifies every unwanted bulge, including those both above and beneath a bra.

 Too tight

'Silk is not often thought of as a wardrobe staple. But I find that basic shapes – a T-shirt for example – in navy or cream silk, looks chic and stylish. All it needs is one piece of jewellery, like pearls, real or fake, or a silver/gold chain necklace to take you from boardroom to family event.' — Suzy Menkes

# Knitwear

At the moment knitwear is fashionable, especially bulky knits, but many knitwear styles are not great if you have any sort of a bosom; again, knitted pieces often look much more elegant if you buy them one size larger than you would normally think of choosing.

Narrow cardigan

# 'A V-neck is often more flattering than a round neck – particularly if you have a larger bosom.'

- A V-neck is often more flattering than a round neck – particularly again if you have a larger bosom. I do have a round neck jumper that I love, but it is based on a man's jumper and quite long and loose.
- If you are slightly thicker around the waist avoid sweaters that are overly fully fashioned or fit too closely; sometimes when you sit down, a tightish sweater can have a tendency to follow the rolls rather too snugly.
- Then there is the boyfriend cardigan: I like them and they look wonderful on the young. But they're not terribly feminine after a certain age; I think they're a bit butch and that a lot of women don't feel particularly comfortable in them. Wear a long cardigan by all means, but choose a narrow shape, more fitted than the boyfriend model, and perhaps worn with a feminine shirt or some jewellery.

Knitted tunic

# Skirts

Skirt lengths are always something to think about: there definitely comes a time, or an age, when any short skirt is a too-short skirt. And, in this context, too short is well above the knee. Apart from anything else, it's really just not terribly sophisticated to walk around with your skirt flapping round your thighs, particularly in your day-to-day life and when you're at home. It's much more elegant to wear a skirt length that either sits on the knee or just below, although that said, if your knees still look ok, a skirt that finishes <u>just</u> above them can work, especially if it is made in a good, not too flimsy material – and if, in the winter, you wear opaque tights, preferably black (see Tights page 72).

✓ *Stitched pleats*

✗ *Difficult dirndl*

# 'Long skirts should NOT be straight; this is not a good look. Instead go for a softer, flowing silhouette – perhaps a soft skirt that grazes the upper calf.'

And, as with other things in my wardrobe, if a skirt is much too short, I do tend to get rid of it and replace it. I can't repeat often enough – you have to be ruthless with your wardrobe, however hard that may be.

Of course you don't have to wear knee-length skirts – if your legs are not your best feature, you might feel far more comfortable in a longer skirt. Long skirts, however, should NOT be straight; this is not a good look. Go for a softer, flowing silhouette – perhaps a soft skirt that grazes the upper calf. If you go for that length, the height of shoe is important – flat heels, high heels or boots. Spanish riding boots with a chunky, stacked heel look good with a fuller skirt.

*Mini skirt*

# 'Never combine an A-line skirt with an A-line top – you will look like a triangle on legs.'

The pleats on a pleated skirt should not fall directly from the waistband, unless you are exceptionally slim or well under 40 – this is an instant stomach disaster. Pleated skirts must either be stitch pleated to hip level or to be cut so that they are flat round the tummy, breaking into pleats below. A possible exception are sunray pleats which, if they are cut fine and narrow over the hips, can <u>sometimes</u> look good on those who are less than slim-hipped.

## A-line skirts

I bought an A-line skirt the other day – a bit dowdy, I have to say. In essence, the A-line is quite a good shape for a lot of women, as it is comfortable to wear and forgiving of lumps and bumps, but it can be unflattering and look unbelievably frumpy. Look carefully at the cut – many A-line styles, particularly an exaggerated or full A-line cut, flare out over the hips and so add to the width, making you look broader – not a desirable look; always look for one that is slim cut below the waist and the hips. If it is not calf-length or longer, an A-line skirt will look best sitting just on the knee – this gives a better proportion than when it is worn above the knee.

These skirts should be worn with neat tops – a fitted T-shirt or jumper, ideally tucked in – although a boxy top is possible. Never combine an A-line skirt with an A-line top – you will look like a triangle on legs.

If your skirt ends just below the knee a flat shoe is possible, but you will usually look and feel more elegant in a medium heel; this is also a style where boots always work, whatever the length of the skirt.

A longer, fuller soft skirt in a lightweight fabric is always pretty when fitted over the hips and finishing at mid-calf. Note though that no-one since Heidi has looked good in a dirndl skirt, they are as unflattering – unless you are VERY slim – as full, pleated skirts.

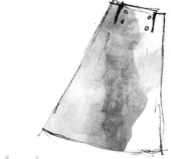

*A-line skirt*

✗ Frumpy.    ✓ Flattering

# Trousers

Ah, trousers – today a fashion given, whatever your age, and worn by everyone, everywhere and at any time. The easy answer to what-to-wear days, you might think, but read on. Personally, I find trousers really difficult. I often see women wearing styles of trouser that are simply too tight; it's not that the women haven't got great figures – they have. But I just don't think that, over a certain age, it works to try and show off your figure – particularly when there are pockets of fat around your waist that bulge over the top of the trousers. This is definitely <u>not</u> a good look.

*Flat fronted*

And here's another reality check: after a certain age, the bottom – your bottom – drops, and even sags, so if you are wearing something that is tight and with a bit of stretch, there is likely to be a very un-gorgeous bum-indentation, which is seriously not a good look at all.

**So – what to look for?**

- The size that you buy will depend on the size of your tummy, for trousers must not clutch your body, either round the sides or round the crotch.
- If your tummy is rather more visible than you might wish, and your thighs a little more pear than perfect, think of buying the next size up; the waist will fit and you will find that the material will be easy across and round the thighs and tummy, giving a much more elegant look.

# And another thing...

I do see a lot of my friends walking round in skin tight leggings or jean-leggings—'jeggings' as they are sometimes called. They're all grandmothers, and they've all got these great figures; there is a group of glamorous grannies who refuse to believe that they are anything other than the same shape and age as their daughters. But jeggings just don't work for me unless the area below the waist and down to the thigh is covered.

# 'The taller you are, the wider you can wear your trousers.'

**Trouser Types**

In the winter, and indeed for much of the year, try a pair of flat-fronted, straight trousers with quite a narrow leg – in principle it is best to avoid pleat-fronts, as pleats, by their very nature, accentuate the tummy. Another shape to avoid is an over-exaggerated stove-pipe leg; easier by far are the straight, cigarette legs that are flattering to both the leg and the foot. It goes without saying that if your shape is less than perfect, lighter-weight materials are more flattering than heavy wools or tweeds.

Personally, I wear straight trousers with a long tunic, a straight-cut, rather than fitted shirt or sweater or a T-shirt with a slightly A-line shape. All good, all flattering and, importantly, all covering the bottom – as well as the crotch – which Must Not Show; tight-fitting trousers that Clutch the Crotch are really unappealing.

A pair of wider than average straight-cut style – and in soft wool or heavy cotton – are flattering, or even men's trousers that are loose in the crotch. Many women think that they don't like and can't wear baggy trousers, but you shouldn't be frightened of them. The one thing to remember about wide trousers is that their width should be balanced with your height – the taller you are, the wider the trousers can be – but as a style they are not only easy to wear, but look great, and pretty sophisticated worn with a cardigan and maybe some jewellery. Try them!

*Leggings*

39

Summer trousers could include straight-cut men's shapes as well as both narrow and wide styles – the latter with a drawstring or elasticated waist, if you prefer. I have a beige and a navy pair (not white) and these more or less get me through the season.

**Trouser length vs Heel Height**

The difference between looking wonderful in trousers and looking quite wrong is often the length. Wide-legged trousers should be long; on average the back of the trouser leg should almost touch the ground. The longer they are, the more elegant, and the taller you will appear.

*Elasticated*

'I wear skirts at home, but always trousers when going out.' — Grace Coddington

A straight, narrower trouser should be hemmed to finish at the top of your instep.

Most women wear their trousers much too short; this is not to say that you should not wear short trousers – but it should be clear that they are a style rather than a mistake. Short trousers should either be very narrow, leg-hugging Capri pants that are designed to be finish on the ankle or slightly above, or they can be slightly wider, and worn with flat or high-heeled shoes. The tie-topped short, wide trouser goes in and out of fashion and is a fun item for a relaxed look.

Culottes, which occasionally have a fashion moment, are a mystery to me; they come into the same category as the even more mysterious body-suits and all-in-one jump suits – all being incredibly difficult to get in and out of.

It is a rule of the really well-dressed that a pair of trousers finished and hemmed to wear with flat shoes cannot be worn with high heels. And vice versa. When you buy a pair of trousers that fit well, you have to make a decision – am I going to wear these trousers with high heels? In which case they have to be one length. Or – am I going to always wear them with flat shoes? In which case they will have to be another length; simples.

And perhaps, if you find a pair of trousers that fit perfectly and look good, you should buy two pairs of the same style and have them hemmed to different lengths so that you can wear them both with flat and high-heeled shoes. I have actually done that, and was very pleased as the perfect pair of trousers can take you so long to find in the first place.

## Leggings

Let's be clear: leggings are really tights with the feet cut off – a style which can never be really flattering, and to me are just a lazy option. They look bad worn on their own, and are never a good look unless you have great legs and a bottom that doesn't sag and then only under a forgiving long top (see below).

I was at supper one evening where the hostess wore a little black dress, and most of the guests were dressed at the same level. One guest arrived wearing skin-tight Lycra jeans, which were really identical to , and as tight as, a pair of leggings – she was 60-something and Juno-esque. I'm afraid I couldn't tear my eyes away from her bottom. It really wasn't her best look.

However, these days leggings are ubiquitous and so, as long as you select the style carefully – and team them with the right top – you can make them work, whatever your body shape. But a few rules apply:

- Never wear them too tight – aim for fitted not clingy.
- Don't choose a fabric that is too thin. This will be far too revealing when stretched over curves, and is reminiscent of a pantomime Principal Boy look – to be avoided at all costs even at Christmas. Remember, when an elasticated fabric is stretched over an uneven body contour it will be most see-through where it is most stretched. If you are not properly covered, underwear can quite clearly be seen – I have witnessed floral pants under black leggings!
- Good underwear is vital.
- Both leggings and, indeed, tight jeans should sit on the waist not the hip, or you will be constantly yanking them up.
- A longer top, whether tunic style or a looser shirt, can cover the tummy and thigh area if disguise is necessary – which more often than not is the case.

'Let's be clear – leggings are really tights with the feet cut off...'

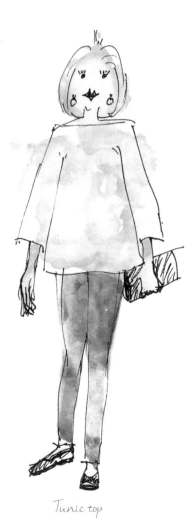

Tunic top

# Jeans

No book of this nature would be complete without some words on jeans. I don't wear them very often myself, but I look around and everyone else seems to wear them a lot – indeed they are an everyday staple. I have been watching people in the street wearing jeans and also in shops trying them on and at the moment almost everyone seems to prefer the skinny variety and the skinnier the better it would seem. However– like T-shirts – jeans change shape every season, sometimes subtly, sometimes more obviously so. At the time of writing, flared jeans are once more appearing, as are a softer version of the baggy boyfriend jean, so it is important you look for a shape and fit that suits you, no matter what the shape of the season might be.

# And another thing...

Straight

Boot flare

Wide

Tight jeans with a shirt tucked in–hmm. If you don't have the waistline just untuck the shirt. Too tight jeans always seem to clutch in the crotch (vulgarly called camel-toe, and you can understand why), and emphasize my less than perfect thighs whilst accentuating my stomach, which these days is not wash-board flat.

# 'The darkest denim is always the most flattering...'

Blue denim comes in many shades as well as white denim – and black of course. White jeans for summer can look great if you are slim, but I would recommend an easy fit and a straight leg. They are great for travelling and for weekends with a variety of tops; the very lightness of white will emphasize size though, so avoid if you are self-conscious about your shape.

If you are sticking to blue denim, the darkest denim available is nearly always the most flattering; actually, after a certain age, darker denim is always more flattering, and smarter, no matter what cut you choose.

The good news on the jeans front is that, as well as whatever is currently modish, there are many, many other styles of jeans on the market, each one carefully designed to fit – and suit – many different body shapes, so it pays to see exactly what is out there before you make your choice.

Bootcut jeans are designed, as you might guess, to fit over a pair of boots and are therefore straight-legged and slightly flared at the bottom of the leg. Always a flattering cut, bootcut jeans are good for balancing out slightly heavier hips or bust; look for a medium or high-rise pair.

Skinny jeans are the narrowest of the jean shapes, fitted in the leg and to the ankle. There are various degrees of skinny – some more so, some less. Needless to say, this is not your style if you have either big hips or tummy or wide calves. They are almost always made from denim that has a degree of stretch in it; watch for this – a slight degree of stretch can make the jeans fit better; too much stretch and the wearer could look as if she has been swaddled in cling film. It may seem contradictory, but when buying skinny or narrow jeans try them on a size larger and see if you don't think you look less pumped up.

High waisted

Straight jeans have no flare in the cut, but neither do they cling to the leg and ankle; they are akin to the boyfriend jean, although the shape of the latter is slouchier and sometimes more comfortable to wear, and is my preferred shape for most women.

In the main the tighter jeans seems to come with low or medium rise waistlines, a disaster for the tummied-ones amongst us. High-rise are the best, but seem very difficult to find, although fashion seems to be coming round to the shape, which may mean they will be more widely available. A rather plump acquaintance of mine who is really round these days swears by maternity jeans with an elasticated front panel, although I do think this may well be the course of last resort.

———

Elasticated pants, sometimes with longer thigh length legs, are often recommended to wear underneath jeans. The thought of this solution under a tight pair of jeans seems very uncomfortable to me and, of course, as with any elasticated piece of underwear, it holds you in one place and distributes the displacement of flesh elsewhere. In the case of jeans, this will be around the waist, creating the dreaded 'muffin top'.

———

———

There's no easy way to find the right pair of jeans – you've got to set aside time and effort. And there is a website (www.donnaida.com) where they do your body shape for you. You measure yourself and then you fill it in and then they put up a little outline of you on screen and then they fit the measure the jean online around you... more

———

I have trawled the internet for words of wisdom and there are many. The best piece of advice was to go to a good shop and employ a personal shopper to prepare a selection for you to try. All good stores offer this service, and for me it is more satisfactory than trying to find jeans online, as more often than not they will have to be sent back at least once.

If you don't want to go down the internet route, nor like the idea of a personal shopper studying your weaker points, the high street does offer an enormous variety of styles of jeans where you can – anonymously – try on styles until you find the right pair for you. Be prepared though to spend quite some time and try on a LOT of different pairs. In the end, buying jeans is a bit of a Princess and the Frog situation – you've got to kiss a lot of blue frogs before you find your denim Prince...

'I don't believe in rights and wrongs when it comes to style. People can look stylish in anything, if they seem to have dressed for themselves rather than to impress anyone else.'

— Dame Harriet Walter

'I have learned over the years that simplicity and comfort are more important than being named on any best-dressed list. When I feel comfortable in a dress I know I will look and feel my best.' — Christy Turlington Burns

# Dresses

If I ever opened a shop it would be for dresses only. In a perfect world I would rather wear nothing but dresses, as they are so easy to wear, the ideal form of clothing – just put one on and go. But, to be honest, they're quite difficult to find, and tracking down the right one can be a problem.

Tunic

If you are going for a cheaper dress, whether it is a winter or summer weight, do try it in several sizes – often a larger size than you would normally wear will look better – and of course if you can find a good-looking dress with sleeves, snap it up!

Don't dismiss dresses with waists, but if the dress of your choice does have a waist, do check that it is not too short-waisted for your height. Try it on before you buy – don't buy from a catalogue or online unless you are absolutely confident in the designer's cut; a dress that sits much above your natural waistline can make you look pregnant and out of proportion.

Wrap

Although they still feature a lot in newspapers and magazines, body-con dresses (those that fit very closely to the shape of the body) and tight-fitting shift dresses, unless they are cleverly made, can be very difficult to wear. These styles need to be forgiving in their design – the shift must not touch the body or it will ride up when you are sitting and standing. They work if they are made in a fabric such as double jersey and if they have gathers or ruching at both front and back.

That said, if you've got a good shape and you're in proportion, no matter what your size, there's no reason why you shouldn't show it off. It's just that it's best not to reveal too much by wearing something that is too tight and skimpy. And don't forget the benefits of a lightweight, long cardigan to soften the line over the tummy.

Yet again, as with tops for trousers and skirts, one style that always works well as a dress, whatever your shape, is a tunic – very often much better than a belted style. Another shape that is deservedly still very popular is the wrap dress – the shape that Diane von Furstenberg first designed and introduced in 1974, variations of which she still produces in different colourways and styles every season. Its success means that there are now many versions available at all price levels and – particularly in a plain colour, rather than a print – they really are very forgiving; the gathers hide the tummy and the V-neck is always flattering. I wear mine a lot, particularly on less confident days.

'Occasionally allow a sales person to persuade you to try something that you wouldn't choose for yourself. The other day I saw a personal-shopper in Selfridges and against my better judgement she encouraged me to try a Diane von Furstenberg tunic which looked like nothing special on the hanger. I bought it and have often worn it, feeling great and always being complimented.' — Sue Crewe

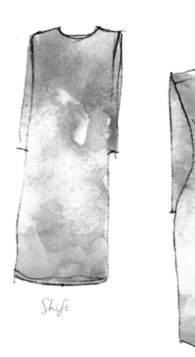

Shift

Bodycon

# Coats and Jackets

The first question on the coat front is how many should you have? I'm afraid that just one will not do – you need different lengths and different shapes. People think their coats will go on forever – but they don't, of course. They lose their shape and the lining frays and disintegrates.

*Princess line*

# 'If your bust is not too large, a semi-fitted princess line, narrow at the top and falling to a fullish skirt, is romantic and flattering...'

Like most people these days, I have more than one coat – about four to date, and I do wear one more than the others. I have a puffa coat for every day as well as a smart waisted black coat for funerals and so on, as well as a trench coat and an edge-to-edge 'town' coat.

Although the accepted rule is that you should buy as expensive a coat as possible, it is actually better to buy one good coat – the one you are going to wear most – and pay less for the others. There are many good coats on the high street, and the key to success there is to find one that is as simple as possible, and comparatively muted in colour. It's the trimmings – the fancy buttons and belts – that make a coat look cheap, so if you really like the coat in every other respect, check that you can change, or discard, the offending elements.

– A down coat with a hood is ideal for bad weather. If you select a smart looking one in black or a dark colour it can see you through from walking the dog to going out for dinner with friends. A decent hood also saves you having to juggle an umbrella – that most annoying of accessories.

– A smart wool coat is a confidence-building garment. If your bust is not too large, a semi-fitted, princess line, fitted at the top, and falling to a fullish skirt is flattering and romantic looking as well as chic. The disadvantages of this style is that it must look fairly fitted when buttoned, and so you can't wear anything too bulky underneath. The second disadvantage is that although any skirt shape will work with a princess line, trousers are, I think, a compete no-no as they should only ever been worn beneath a straight, un-fitted coat – either long or short.

'When you try a jacket on for the first time, bring both hands forward to test the fit across the back and shoulders to see whether it is too tight or will not hang properly...'

- As far as colour goes, if you are only buying one coat, it is sensible to steer away from bright colours as you, and others, can easily get bored with too much colour. (Unless your heart is set on bright red, and you have the budget to be extravagant and self-indulgent – it is always an uplifting colour!) Navy is the most versatile and softer than black; grey and camel are possibilities – but choose the latter only if it suits your complexion (see page 97).
- A light coat or mac (see trench coats, page 97) should be on standby – long enough, but not too long, to work with both skirts and trousers.

## Jackets for the Day

Jackets are the most useful of garments and can change, formalize or immediately update a basic outfit of trousers, dress or skirt in a moment, as well as adding an element of dressed-up-ness when required. I have a wardrobe of jackets, although I don't keep them for ever, rather buying them and then discarding after a few seasons. Like everything else in your wardrobe, just because you've had a particular jacket for years, doesn't mean it still looks good when you wear it now.

When you try on a jacket for the first time, bring both hands forward to test the fit across the back and shoulders. If it pulls uncomfortably or starts to wrinkle under the arms, then it is too tight and will not hang properly. And always check in a two-sided mirror before buying.

## Jacket Styles

### The Peacoat
Based on the traditional seaman's coat , the
modern peacoat is a classic style – usually navy,
always double breasted, buttoning to the collar
if needed, and usually hip length. They are
smart – they look good with trousers – and are
also very adaptable; best of all, the straight (or
sometimes slightly fitted) lines of the peacoat
are remarkably flattering for all shapes.

*Soft*

### The Blazer
The blazer is usually considered a classic in the
modern wardrobe. Historically the province
of rowing teams and later generations of
schoolchildren, the almost-suit jacket, single or
double breasted and with lapels, encompasses
many variations on the theme, and a style
for every woman. For those of small frame,
cropped, single breasted and fitted works well;
for taller women, a longer, straighter cut with
structured shoulders looks good. A blazer
works both in summer and winter weights, and
is an useful part of any wardrobe, particularly
in navy and a summer neutral shade.

*Blazer*

Box

### The Boxy Jacket

A boxy jacket is good with an A-line skirt and an edge-to-edge, collarless jacket of varying length, and in a variety of materials, goes over anything, from narrow trousers to a summer or winter dress and also combines very well with jewellery, so works well dressed up for the evening.

### The Biker Jacket

This may not be everyone's first choice when thinking about jackets, as the wrong style and cut can look a bit 'fashion-victim' when worn on someone over the age of 30, but if worn in a fabric – rather than in chrome-studded and buckled black leather – I rather like this shape. It works in the same way as a short, fitted jacket and can fill the same role rather neatly and in a modern way, particularly with straight trousers and skirts.

Biker

'Velvet, in all its plush gorgeousness has been worn for centuries by queens (and kings). It is a rich seam to plunder for night and day.' — Suzy Menkes

### General Jacket Tips

Summer dressing always needs a jacket – a good navy one and a neutral or white one too, if possible.

- I would always choose a simple, slightly fitted, slightly longer blazer style, but on a slimmer figure a shorter jacket or one with a peplum can also look good.
- An unstructured, unlined and soft shape is another jacket option which sometimes works well over simple dresses, shirts and skirts, etc.
- Box or short jackets work far better over dresses and skirts than trousers – personally with trousers I always wear a longer jacket to cover my rear.
- Remember, whatever shape jacket you choose, always check the final outfit from the back.

### Jackets in the Evening

Many people own a velvet jacket – usually slightly waisted, sometime with a peplum and stand-up collar and often with frogging. They are quite pretty (although usually worn a bit too short) – but only when they are new. If you've had a jacket like that since you were 25, you really need to replace it. Your bottom might be bigger, ditto your bust and the shape of a soft-fabric jacket like this will have long gone – the hem will be curling up, and there will be worn patches. Get a new one, and this time round make sure that it is long enough.

# 'Don't think that the tuxedo jacket that you bought in the 1980s and is still sitting in the back of the wardrobe is going to work – it won't.'

The same goes for the Indian-inspired narrow quilted jackets and coats: they can look quite nice, particularly if they have a stand-up collar, but *only* when they are new. Sagging quilted cotton or wool is not a good look.

One of the most useful versatile of evening jackets is a black tuxedo – definitely something that has a lot of style as well as being multi-useful. But please don't think that the one with the big shoulders that you bought in the 1980s and which is still sitting at the back of the wardrobe is going to work; actually it's just going to immediately draw attention to the fact that it's old and that you have changed. Extremes are not what you're going for, just something that looks great. Don't agonise about it, just give it to your daughter or one of your friend's daughters – she may make it work for herself, but you can go out and buy a new one.

'I like to wear narrow trousers, flat shoes and well-tailored jackets. Shirts should end at the lower hip or slightly below, covering the crotch. My skirts are to the upper calf.' — Grace Coddington

'My wardrobe has many pieces of classical clothing that I love – classical jackets, trousers, pullovers, beautiful shirts, simple well-cut lines mostly in plain colours.'

— HRH Princess Michael of Kent

# Shoes

Shoes equal feet in this context – many women just don't look at their feet enough, if ever, and simply don't realize that feet can very quickly become ugly. As our feet age they become wider, and the bones at the sides can start to protrude. Although there is not too much you can easily do about the physical changes, I promise you that a good pedicure is an instant short-term solution and worth its weight and cost in gold. Every woman should have one – and preferably more often than once at Christmas and once before a summer holiday.

*Classic courts.*

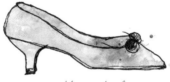

*Kitten heel*

*Slip-on/Slide*

*Daytime sandals*

Avoid nail polish colours like orange, purple, black (please – no) and candy floss pink; by far the best colour for the toenails is red – it flatters both feet and toes, whether they are tanned or not, and makes them look years younger. Like a gift-wrapped present, a good pedicure makes the contents look even nicer.

# *And another thing...*

Personally, I don't like shoes with leather soles at all; they are very slippery and also they absorb water. Any boot or shoe that I buy with a leather sole I take straight to the cobbler to have a ridged rubber sole put on, both to stop me slipping and also to stop water destroying the sole.

Onto the pedicured feet come the shoes and the first thing to say about shoes is, look after them! Keep them on shoe trees, and please, polish them.

And don't keep them for too long, the exception being brogues – an old pair of brogues or moccasins is wonderful, and look better with time – but five-year old navy or black court shoes in soft leather will not look very good, no matter how cared for they have been – the shape goes; shapeless shoes are VERY ageing.

If you wear the same pair of shoes endlessly, the heel starts sloping inwards and that looks so bad – as if you are far too lazy to have the shoes heeled. It is extraordinary that people don't notice that more about their shoe wardrobe.

## Shoe Styles

A shoe wardrobe should include different styles of flat shoe, from ballet pumps to slipper styles and loafers – which look great with wide or mannish trousers and also with skirts and dark opaque tights, although they do look rather heavy with bare legs, unless they are of very soft leather.

Flat shoes are fashionable now – thank goodness – which means that you can find beautiful shoes in all colours and materials from satin to leather, so it is time to think of them as the smart, rather than the easy, scruffy option kept by the back door. By all means have a couple of old pairs for scruff wear, but treat other flat shoes with as much respect as those with heels – which means shoe trees and shoe cream.

Ballet pumps are a brilliant staple; two pairs, one in black and one in tan will cover winter and summer. Not all ballet pumps are equal though – they should be low-cut, otherwise they make the feet look big, but they mustn't be TOO low-cut, otherwise there will be too much toe cleavage – not a good look. So shopping around is a good idea.

The slide, with a rubber sole, is cut higher up the foot and has become more popular over the last few years. It is easy to wear and often looks more modern with trousers than a ballet pump.

The slipper (called this because it is based on a man's bedroom slipper), which is cut higher up the foot but is lighter than a loafer, has become more popular over the last couple of years, is easy to wear and again, like the slide, often looks newer and more contemporary with trousers than a ballet pump.

Ballet pump

Slipper

'There is a moment when every wise woman wants to step out of agonizingly uncomfortable shoes. Why not kitten – rather than killer – heels?' — Suzy Menkes

'Shoes need to be discreet and flattering – old feet can be very unattractive!' — Diana Donovan

# 'For the evening, one pair of elegant high heel shoes – perhaps in black satin – are a staple, because they make you feel better...'

### A Word about Heel Height

– During the day, low heels work well – as I say I am a great fan of the kitten heel as well as the low block heel, both of which work equally well with skirts and trousers. For the evening, one pair of elegant high heel shoes – perhaps in black satin – are a staple, because they make you feel better; they needn't be very high, just higher than you might wear in the day. Higher heels also make you stand better: heels push the body up and back, and that's good for both your deportment and your confidence.

– For summer I like flat shoes, ballet pumps or similar, plimsolls, espadrilles and sandals – which should either be flat or with a squat heel. But although flat shoes are both fashionable and so much more comfortable than shoes with heels, particularly in warm weather, there are occasions when a heel is essential. On summer evenings silver or gold sandals – the lazy solution – work for me every time whether they are flat or high-heeled sandals; and because I wear them less frequently, they can go on for quite some time.

*Kitten sandal*

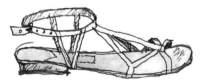

*Flat metallic sandal*

# Boots

As with coats, so with boots; more than one pair is definitely needed – ideally you would have two or three different pairs, which would include a flat pair for everyday to wear with skirts and over narrow trousers; a knee-height pair with heels for wearing on smarter occasions or with trousers; and ankle boots for straighter, shorter trousers.

# 'Ankle boots are not the most flattering of styles if you don't have great legs; the answer here is to look for a pair that is wide at the ankle and easy to get on and off...'

- Not everyone's calves fit into narrow cut boots, so look for those with zips or elasticated sides, as well as Spanish-style riding boots – which are wide and with a low or stacked heel; they look good with a fuller skirt.
- Ankle boots are very popular and they do look great with a slightly longer skirt and worn with opaque tights;. they are not, however, the most flattering of styles if you don't have great legs; the answer here is to look for a pair that are wide at the ankle and are easy to get on and off.
- A low, classic Chelsea boot with insets of elastic at the sides that you can wear under trousers also looks good and will not date.

Flat boots can be worn with almost anything; the riding boot style, which works best in soft, dark leather, will work well with a winter ethnic look, or equally with a country look.

*Ankle*

*Country*

# *And another thing...*

Don't reject the idea of wearing boots to and from your destination and taking shoes to change into once you get there. When I started with Russian *Vogue* I picked up the habit of changing and leaving my boots with my coat; everyone does it there for obvious reasons, and it makes life so much easier.

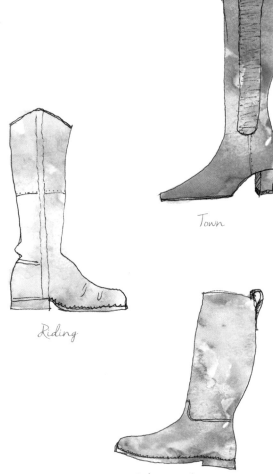

Town

Riding

Wet weather

'I can no longer wear heels and wear slides instead, even in the evening (slip-one with a thick, white sole and a variety of uppers).'

— Grace Coddington

'Large feet need simple, plain styles so as not to draw attention; smaller feet can have a selection like that of Madame Marcos! If only!' — HRH Princess Michael of Kent

# Tights

The first thing to say about tights is that wearing the wrong tights – wrong texture, colour, tone – is very ageing. Now read on:

– At the first signs of spring, winter-weight, opaque tights somehow seem heavy and inappropriate. Of course it would be so liberating to just decide not to wear any tights at all, but unless you have exceptional skin and legs – and a bit of colour – this is simply not an option.

# 'For some reason, flesh tights are taboo in the fashion world; no-one would wear them – except me.'

- For some reason, flesh tights are taboo in the fashion world; no-one would wear them – except me. I buy very, very sheer (low denier) light-tan coloured tights each spring because I feel so much more comfortable in them than in bare legs; even though they are sheer they still smooth out the skin tone, making it look good and hiding imperfections, of which I seem to have more as my legs age. If you already have a favourite brand of tights, that's fine – just be sure to choose ones that are sheer enough (almost invisible) and in a shade that tones with the rest of your body.

- As summer goes on so my legs seem to improve in texture and colour and I feel brave enough to venture out bare-legged. That pedicure is now essential as I have already said, go for a clear red or dark–red coloured polish, although natural toes – either finished with clear polish or filed and buffed to a shine – are fine as long as they are properly looked after.
- If you like wearing sandals, they do NOT work with tights – ever – so the above advice is pretty essential. However, you can get toeless tights to wear with open-toed shoes. I've tried them: they do work well, although you must always check that there is no tell-tell edge of tight showing through the open toe.

- Winter legs are definitely easier: I am a big fan of opaque tights – they disguise most defects from thick ankles to hairy legs and I wear them almost daily during the winter, which is lazy, I admit, but it works and is fairly effortless. In the evening I think that natural, very sheer tights are the chicest choice, but black sheer tights also look very good.

- I usually buy opaque tights a size larger than usual so that the colour is even all over the leg, rather than becoming paler where they are being stretched i.e. over the knees. Tights with a shine tend to make the legs look fatter, whereas matt tights make them look slimmer. The only exception, I think, is in high summer when a slight sheen on sheer natural tights gives a more natural look.

- If your style is a bit boho, then, I think, coloured tights can be fun sometimes, although they are difficult to get right, looking a bit off unless they are teamed with the right outfit – and personally, I am never quite sure what that outfit might be. Striped, lacy or decorative tights look great on the young, but they are not for me.

If you wear trousers a lot in the winter then those very unattractive pop sox are perfect as no-one sees them, but do make sure they are long enough – the sight of an elasticated top when you are sitting down is not a good look. As far as colour goes the same rules apply as for tights – matt black for day and natural or sheer black for evening. If you are not wearing black shoes, socks can work, but only in neutral shades such as grey or camel.

'I usually buy opaque tights a size larger than usual so that the colour is even all over the leg, rather than becoming paler where they are being stretched over the knees...'

## And another thing...

On the subject of ageing summer feet – and by extension, ageing summer legs – because I now wear glasses I kid myself there is no stubble, although when I run my hand up my leg, there it is, which means that all those who don't need glasses, can see it. So be regular with maintenance, whether it be waxing, depilation or shaving.

Personally I only apply fake tan on my legs for important outings as I find it so boring to apply on a daily basis as well as being difficult to apply without patches and streaks, but if you find it easy, then by all means, use it – just be sure to avoid dark patches around knees, ankles and toes.

# Handbags

I don't spend money on a new bag each season, although many people do. I tend to get attached to a good and useful bag and go on using it till it starts to look like a deflating balloon. Professionals say that you should switch bags on a regular basis in order to maintain their shapes, but I am too idle to transfer things on a daily basis from one bag to another just to suit what I am wearing; the result is one bag which goes on for years, definitely looking slightly the worst for wear over time. Bags cost a fortune and I am rather mean, so I prefer to make do with one or two long-lasting shapes, but even I will change these before they become an embarrassment.

Clutch

Travel

Ideally, though, I believe one *should* have several bags. A big tote for travel, and smaller handbag for lunch dates, and one or two evening bags. The larger tote could be in black – practical – although it could be bright red as red goes well with most things – less practical, possibly, but the colour is more fun.

Inside the tote you would usually keep a smaller bag for all the little things like make-up, credit card holder, etc – one which can be zipped up and attached to the main tote for safety. Choose one with a zip or with a zip compartment inside for travel documents, etc.

'For holidays I always pack a small collapsible cloth bag to take to the beach or pool or even to supper. I have even been known to use a fabric shoe bag when in a spot...'

- Shoulder bags with a long strap are not as popular as they were, but they are very practical as they are secure and leave both hands free for other things; try wearing them with the strap shortened, or diagonally across the body. The cross-body bag is perhaps the modern shoulder bag equivalent and there are numerous styles and sizes to try.
- In winter a black bag is essential for most people, or at least a navy or brown one. In summer tan is a good, smart colour and I like red for both seasons.
- For holidays I always pack a small collapsible cloth bag to take to the beach or pool or even to dinner if it is informal. I have even been known to use a fabric shoe bag when in a spot. Somehow a smart leather bag looks out of place in informal sunny locations.

- For the evening I think a small bag looks elegant. A black or dark clutch is probably the obvious staple, but a bag that is beaded or in silver or gold is very useful both in winter and summer, and there are many cheap, pretty designs on the high street. A lot of small bags come with an optional shoulder chain or strap – useful for drinks parties when one has to juggle both a glass and a canapé.

# And another thing...

I have a shelf of beautiful bags accumulated over the years and hardly worn except on high days. The result is that they are all in perfect condition and will last forever. Some shapes are dated now, but I still treasure the bags because they are beautiful, chosen at the time because I loved them – and, after all, they may well, one day, be fashionable again.

# Accessories

### Scarves

I've never been a scarf person but I do have a couple of large, soft pashmina-type scarves, which are incredibly useful for travel and very cold weather. I have quite a lot of black clothes and as I now realize that black is not the most becoming colour as one ages, I find that bright scarves, either in fine wool or a wool and cotton mix rather than silk, are very good at brightening and softening an outfit, as well as framing your face.

Scarves shouldn't be tied too tightly or too neatly. I usually wear them by twisting them once loosely round the neck and then tying them in front so that there are not too many trailing ends.

As far as shape goes look for long rectangles rather than squares which, at the moment, look old-fashioned. Don't get rid of the latter, just don't wear them now. Like belts, scarf shapes always come back into fashion – eventually.

'If finding the right clothes for an occasion is difficult, choose a great scarf, earrings or necklace to enhance your image.' — Joan Burstein

## Hats

Hats no longer seem essential except when specified, as at formal race meetings such as Royal Ascot. Although most people still wear hats at weddings, I have noticed recently that more and more women go bare-headed, or wear an excuse for a hat, such as a decorated Alice band or similar.

- A favourite hat can be refreshed with a new ribbon or pin, but be sure that the hat is worth it; if it looks a bit tired, buy a new one.
- Department stores are good hat-hunting grounds, with designer ranges at high street prices, and sometimes vintage shops come up with finds.
- Even hiring a hat seems a good idea to me, although it is expensive.
- I am not a great fan of fascinators, but they are the answer to many women's hat issues – they are easy to transport, and all you have to worry about is securing them firmly.

# And another thing...

I have quite a large head and so buying off-the-peg hats is difficult because nothing fits – and I can assure you from personal experience that too small a hat will give you a headache! (I have, in desperation, cut the hat beneath the hatband or even the hatband but if the hat has a brim, it will lose its shape when jammed onto your head.)

## Belts

For most, belts are an essential part of the accessory wardrobe, but the size of the belt is important. To wear a wide belt you must be slim, so that there are no tell-tale rolls of flesh above the belt.

A narrow belt can be great to define a waist on a dress. When it works with your proportions, and is not cinched in too tight – nor left too loose and dangling – but just following the lines of your waist, it can be flattering on fuller figures as well as slim ones. Rather than a belt entirely made of leather, an elasticated belt with a leather front and buckle can be more forgiving – it won't dig in and create an unattractive pouch of flesh – definitely not flattering! Soft tie belts, on the other hand, are forgiving on most waists. And as with scarves, always keep your belts, even if you are not wearing a particular style at the moment – the shapes slip in and out of fashion on a periodical basis.

While flat-fronted trousers are better without a belt, manly trousers are better with, particularly – obviously – if they have belt loops.

✕  Unbelted          ✓  Belted

# Jewellery

I am all for jewellery of all types and styles and when you're feeling self conscious about your chins and saggy bits and so on, wear an amazing necklace and people will look straight at that, not at you.

- The same applies to earrings – I consider earrings to be as important as mascara - and whether they are semi-precious drop earrings, classic small gold hoops, diamond studs, or – of course – pearl earrings, which can, almost literally, light up the face, they will always attract attention – in a good way. And costume jewellery earrings can have an amazing, instantaneous effect.
- A gold chain with or without a drop or the same chain in silver is useful when you want something understated
- Equally classic is a gold or silver chain worn on the wrist. This is smartest when worn on over or beside a watch.

# 'You can mix single-stone necklaces together if they are one or two-stranded, or wear them at the same time as one or two chains...'

## Pearls

I adore pearls: I think they are the most beautiful things and I don't want to stop anyone wearing them, but I just think a bit more imagination is needed about when to wear them, as worn in the wrong way, they can be ageing.

The way to wear pearls is not only to wear them in the traditional way, in fact *not* to wear them in the traditional way, but to wear them less formally and team them with the unexpected – a T-shirt and jeans, perhaps, or a summer dress.

## Costume Jewellery

I love costume jewellery; I absolutely adore shopping for fun necklaces, bracelets and earrings to wear on holiday and at the weekend. There is the thrill of the chase: shops of course, but also such fertile hunting grounds such as car-boot sales, school bazaars and the like – they are all full of wonderful, unexpected and unusual things that will give last year's dress, top or shirt a new lease of life. It is what it is, quite obviously not the real thing, so there is no reason to feel that you have to make excuses for it. Just enjoy it.

## Rethinking Antique Jewellery

Many people inherit the odd piece of jewellery from someone in the family, and judging from programmes like the Antiques Road Show, it is also fair to say that many people then never wear the inherited piece, thinking them old-fashioned, ugly or inappropriate.

But antique jewellery has a history, a past, so if you have lovely pieces of old jewellery, try to wear them:
- Brooches are coming back into fashion and can be worn traditionally, alone or – more interestingly – in clusters of two or three on a jacket lapel or on a dress.
- Single gemstones on chains are quite often found in people's jewellery boxes and these look very pretty worn with a V-neckline, either on their own or mixed with other chains and drops, which again immediately looks more up-to-date.
- You can mix single-stone necklaces together if they are one or two-stranded, or wear them at the same time as one or two chains. And single-stone necklaces can work to pick out the colour in an outfit – amethyst and aquamarine look pretty with summer dresses, sapphire and garnets with deeper winter colours.

85

And if you really dislike the style of the piece, consider having the stones reset or the piece altered in some way – much better, surely, to wear it in a new form than never wear it all.

- a single stone might make a lovely ring
- multiple stones can be made into a heavy clasp to attach to a chunky chain or rope of pearls
- many a brooch can be transformed with the addition of a chain attached to each side of the piece, to make it into a striking necklace
- necklaces themselves can be shortened or altered with two catches so that they can be worn at different lengths

There are many jewellers who specialize in restoring and re-setting old gems in imaginative ways and if you are travelling to India – as long as you have a clear idea of the design you want – jewellers there will reset your otherwise unloved pieces at competitive prices.

So go through your old jewel boxes, get everything out and re-assess it – either for yourself or with someone else in mind.

# And another thing...

## A Good Watch

In the fashion world watches themselves have, these days, taken centre stage; they are as prone to fashion trends as changing hemlines. However the fact is that many of us still have one that we have had since our 21$^{st}$ birthday, or even since we were at school, and we see little reason to change it. If that is what you feel, look at whether the watch might look better with a change of strap shape – sometimes that will instantly bring what might seem an old-fashioned watch up-to-date.

Of course a new watch is not strictly essential nor even necessary, but it is an exciting purchase and can bring an outfit up-to-date. A chunky man's watch looks better with jeans and trousers than a smaller, 'ladies' version. Next time somebody asks you what you want as a gift rather than say you don't need anything, suggest a new watch!

Brooches can be pinned to a hat or a belt – my daughter wore a diamond brooch on the sash of her wedding dress and I have worn the same pin attached to ropes of pearls so that it looks like a large clasp worn off-centre rather than at the back of the neck.

# Good Grooming

Since you are presently thinking about the way to wear clothes in order to look your best, do not forget the power of good grooming – a subject that we were drilled on when much younger but which is possibly even more important now!

A friend of mine, who has just turned 70, told me the other day that she felt she wanted a make-up lesson; her hair is now grey, her colouring has changed, and she feels that the make-up she's been wearing for 40 years just isn't doing her any favours any more. I think she's right – at certain stages in your life you should have a make-up lesson or even a make-up demonstration at your preferred make-up counter of a shop or department store; the beauticians are generally very well trained, and actually very good. Of course you may hate what they do, but equally you may come out of it with at least one good idea.

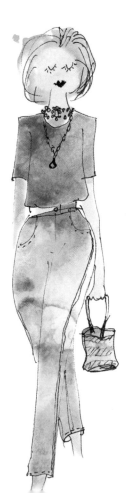

'The key to natural-looking hair is make sure it's cut well in a flattering style – even if your husband prefers you looking the way you were. Many women make that mistake.' — Joan Burstein

- Generally speaking, as you get older, less is more in make-up terms – particularly foundation, which should be as light-textured as possible; a tinted moisturiser can work much better in the daytime. Probably stay away from bright red lipstick; Linda Evangelista, the super-model, told me that after a certain age, your lipstick colour during the day should be no stronger than the colour of the inside of your bottom lip.
- Although too much eye make-up is ageing, using mascara or having your eyelashes dyed can be a huge help (in fact I would put mascara on my list of Ten Essentials You Can't live Without).
- And obviously in the evening you can and should wear more make-up than during the day, although that does not mean heavy foundation, rather an emphasis on lips, eyes and perhaps a bit of judicious blusher.

And a word on hair – the older you get the more important it is to have a good haircut. Hair can get thinner as you age, so a shaped cut that is soft around the face and finishes at the shoulder can be more flattering than when it is left, uncut, to grow in its own way and perhaps become straggly and limp. If you have always worn your hair pulled back check that it is not now too severe; apply the three-way mirror test to both profiles, particularly checking out any signs of a sagging chin.

# Wise words from Well-dressed Women...

'I think beauty is feeling good about yourself, having confidence and spending the time to make yourself the most beautiful you can be. My grandmother Estée always said "if you are beautiful inside, you are beautiful on the outside." She had a belief that every woman could be beautiful if she just spent the time. She said just by taking care of your skin, putting on a little perfume, a little blush, a good moisturizer, you can be beautiful, and I think that philosophy is very important today.' — Aerin Lauder

'We spend too much of our youth dressing to impress our peers, or attract men, to demonstrate our memebrship to some kind of clan, class or type, or worrying about how we are perceived. It is liberating to get older and dress to suit one's own mood, in the colour that feels right to me today. Fabrics become more important than fashion. Comfort becomes more important than perfect elegance. Put it like this, I don't ever again want to wear shoes I can't run for a bus in.' — Dame Harriet Walter

# Working through your Wardrobe

So now that you have digested the previous section about what you should – and shouldn't – have in your wardrobe in general terms, it is time to assess the actual content in more detail. Much has been written by others about the need to go through your wardrobe on a regular basis and get rid of things that you don't wear and haven't worn for a while. It's not easy, but it is essential – edit, edit, edit. Allow some time and get everything out of cupboards and shelves – not all at once, if you can't face it – but make the time to study in forensic detail all of your current clothes situation.

We all have it – that hoarding instinct – and it never leaves you, no matter what your age; so, as with much-loved books, the contents of your larder, and shelves of old china, it's quite likely that, on the clothes front, you have rather more of everything than you thought.

You'll probably find that in stored-away clothes you have any number of variations on several themes – we are all creatures of habit and everyone tends to buy and keep certain items that are basically the same (although they don't necessarily recognize it at the time), such as black trousers, straight skirts, moccasins and court shoes.

It is quite likely that some of the skirts in particular will possibly have shiny and baggy seats, the trousers too. The shoes may have become tight, missshapen and with scuffed heels. So it is important that anything – shirt, skirt, jacket, trousers – that you are not quite sure about, you should try on, and if still in doubt, chuck out. Of course, it's easy to say, but be ruthless here, and if you really can't bear to do it yourself, you can pay a professional wardrobe editor to come to you and go through your wardrobe for you; there's nothing like paying out good money to follow a professional's recommendations.

Moccasin

Court

## And another thing...

Clearing for Cash
There are now savvy wardrobe mistresses who will come to your home, go through your wardrobe with you and take away any discards that they think they can sell on eBay; they take a percentage of what they get for the garment, you never see the clothes again and have an enhanced bank balance into the bargain. That must be worth it.

One well-known British wardrobe editor, Vanessa de Lisle, recommends throwing away anything that you haven't worn for two years, but I think that's too soon – particularly with simply cut clothes. I think you know, in your heart, when you're not going to wear something again, and you must just take the plunge. She's the expert though.

# Classic Fashion... What is it?

As you regard your wardrobe, I hope now with an unjaundiced and clear eye, you will of course keep in mind that every woman needs a wardrobe of basic classics. I have noticed that many people seem to think that classics are called classics because they are clothes that they've had since the 1970s and that's why they can still wear them. Wrong on all counts! You <u>must</u> update your classic pieces – iconic styles they might always have been, but shoulders change, lengths change and, most importantly, your shape changes.

# 'One way of updating classic shapes is to buy them again, but in modern fabric – which will automatically bring the shape more up-to-date...'

Take length – a short jacket might have suited you back in the day, but now you may well need a longer jacket – the hips and the rear may not be as neat as they were. Try on all your short jackets, those with buttons and those without; turn around, find that three-way mirror, ask a friend – is it really still flattering?

And then there are those designs and styles that have achieved almost reverential stature over the years: the camel coat is a good example. We have all been told, through the years, that a camel coat is an investment, something every woman should own, and many of us have bought one at some stage in our fashion lives. But the real truth is that camel not only doesn't suit everyone, it can be a really terrible shade for a western complexion, draining the skin of colour and warmth – not a desirable effect. Is it possibly time to get rid of yours?

Ditto the trench coat – a perennial on those staple lists – but a perennial that is definitely not for everyone. You buy it in one size, then wear it with a sweater and it's immediately too small; a cinched-in waist is certainly not for everyone, neither is the belted-at-the back look. I did own two trenches, one beige and the other black, the latter being rather depressing to my mind – a bit Cruella de Vil really – and it tended to sit in the wardrobe, unworn. Which brings me to the fact that one way of updating classic shapes is to buy them again, but in a modern fabric – which will automatically make the shape more up-to-date.

**Wardrobe Essentials**

Everyone likes a list, so we have compiled a list of classic wardrobe basics around, and on top of which, you can build.

### Coats – Several

One coat in the winter that goes over the top of everything; an easy coat that is knee length and possibly double-breasted as well as a jacket that works with a longer skirt, since although you can wear a skirt that is longer than the coat, it's quite an art to get the look and the proportions right. Possibly a trench coat if you like wearing them (see previous page). The trench coat is a perfect example of the new classic, made in different fabrics and these days, a universal shape. The only caveat, which is important, is that trenches usually look better belted, and not everyone is comfortable with belted coats (again see previous page).

### Jackets

A double breasted pea jacket in either navy or black; look for one that is long enough to cover your bottom and that can be closed at the neck. A blazer in a lighter fabric than that of the pea jacket that can take you through the in-between seasons.

### Black Trousers

Straight legged and narrow. If you wear trousers you should have several styles – smart ones which might be in gabardine or wool crepe, informal trousers which might be of cotton or denim; and for the evening, perhaps a loose jersey pair. Evening trousers always work better in dark colours.

### White Shirt or Two

In a variety of fabrics – particularly cotton, silk and linen.

'The most stylish women are those who appear to be comfortable in their appearance. It's worth building up a collection of failsafe pieces and then sprinkling seasonal stardust into them.' — Alex Shulman

### Tops

For winter a fine cashmere tunic sweater, for summer a good-quality heavy cotton striped, Breton-style elbow-length top in several colours. A tunic top will also be indispensable in a summer wardrobe. Cardigans are always useful to cover short sleeves or simply to keep one warm in changing weather.

### Flat and Low Shoes

Loafers, ballet pumps, slippers or all three.

### Heels

A good pair of low heels for the day and a black suede pair for the evening.

### Straight or A-line skirt

In plain colours and mid-weight fabric with a length that is on or just below the knee. A long evening skirt in jersey is useful - I have a soft one on an elasticated waistband. On top you could wear a tunic, an opaque white shirt or even a twinset – with of course some jewellery if the occasion demands.

### Dress

A Diane von Furstenberg wrap dress or similar. Flattering and easy to wear, the V neck is good if you have a large bosom. Plus a straight shift dress, with or without sleeves, can be dressed up with a scarf, cardigan or jewellery.

### Accessories

For day a bucket or tote bag to throw everything in, big enough to take laptop, with internal pockets for phone and purse. It must sit comfortably on the shoulder and must have some sort of closure so it can't be dipped into. A clutch bag for evening.

### Jewellery

Earrings, necklace or chain.

### Other Bits

Scarves – fine cotton for summer, a long cashmere one for winter. A scarf is a good way to use print to add a bit of colour to an otherwise simple outfit.

# Looking after your Wardrobe

## Hats

Good hats can be expensive; if you have the space, try to keep them in boxes, the hats stuffed with tissue to help them keep their shape. Don't put too many in one box, and then jam on the lid. (I have done this many times and found when I want to wear one, it comes out of the box looking like a lumpy cushion.) Steaming of course helps restore the shape, but you have to be pretty dedicated to the cause to keep the steam coming each time the safety switch turns the kettle off. And don't do this at the last minute – the steam will wreck your hair, and your make-up.

## Tailored Clothes

- Jackets need the most care: they should be hung up immediately you take them off rather than being dumped on a chair. They should also be dry-cleaned regularly – particularly summer jackets which garner all manner of stains that don't show up on heavier winter fabrics. And if they get damp from a rain shower they will need pressing before you wear them again.
- In lieu of a separate storage area where out-of-season clothes can be kept, and in order to keep them clean and in good condition, winter jackets should be bagged for the summer and vice versa.
- Sometimes the lining of a jacket will start to split; if the jacket is good, consider having it relined; the results can be impressive.

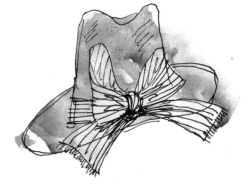

## Shoes

Perhaps the most important point on leather shoe care is to polish them. Please do – too few people do and it is a mistake. And please use shoe trees – they lengthen the life of every pair of shoes.

For some reason if a pair of shoes – usually a pair of classic courts – is not actually falling apart, many women think that they can make do, get by and go on wearing them. You can't; perhaps an old pair of heavy brogues might look good, even improve, with age, but as we have said before, soft leather court shoes certainly do not improve – the shape goes, the toes turn up, and any stray foot bulges show. This is a very ageing look.

# What to Wear with What

Of course, it is something we all think about, when looking at our wardrobes – will this go with this? Can I put these pieces togethe? Will they work? It is not that easy to give specific guidance as it does take a very confident dresser to successfully mix wildly differing styles. Although I have always admired women who do the unexpected with a measure of success, it is quite easy to get it wrong, so my basic advice is start with what you know you wear well, and then push the look a bit further.

'Since jeans are essentially sporty, any jewellery that you wear should be bold and uncomplicated – a man's watch, a cuff, simple earrings or a modern, easy necklace...'

**Jeans**

- The perennial staple, jeans can be worn both informally and semi-formally – dressed-up jeans are quite French-chic.
- If you are dressing them up, it goes without saying, they must be freshly washed (but ironed without creases!).
- Wear them with a T-shirt, blazer and sneakers at the weekend, a winter heavy cashmere and boots, or – at a lunch – with a beautiful shirt or blouse, high heels or sandals.
- Since jeans are essentially sporty, any jewellery that you wear should be bold and uncomplicated – a man's watch, a cuff or wide bangle, simple earrings, or an easy, modern necklace – not all at once, though.

Smart narrow

- Some jeans look great belted, although the skinnier they are, the less the belt is necessary. Like jewellery for jeans, the best belts to choose are those which veer towards the simple rather than the fancy.
- I prefer high-rise jeans as they hide a multitude of bulgy sins. Hipsters never seem to work very well unless you are reed-thin. Nothing ever stays tucked in with low-rise styles and belts only accentuate all the bad points. But if you have a great figure then a belt on waisted jeans looks good.

Straight

'Cropped trousers can look great, but they must be narrow or straight and you must have the confidence to wear them just above the ankle, not higher or lower.'

### Skirts

- Straight, pencil skirts look good with tunic tops and with tight knits (if you have the figure). The straight tunic top in varying lengths is very forgiving and I wear it all the time. No-one can tell what is going on underneath.
- Twin sets too look good with most skirts. They should not be too fitted – à la the 1950s, which looks very dated. Almost all twinsets benefit from a great necklace – preferably not pearls, the combination now being a bit frumpy. Having said that, Chanel gets away with that look every season and it looks wonderful!
- Flared or full skirts should be worn with fitted tops to balance the silhouette – try a peplum jacket or a short jacket that stops at the waist. As with everything check your look from the back before striding out.

### Trousers

Although for most of us trousers are such a staple that we think we probably know how to wear them in a way to suit ourselves, it is important to remember, as I have said before, that they must be the right length for the style. Cropped trousers, for example, can look great, but they must be narrow or straight and you must have the confidence to wear them just above the ankle – not higher, or lower.

*Flared*

- The classic trouser with a longer jacket or blazer (trouser suit) is still a favourite, comfortable look, particularly for women who work in a man's world. But rather than wearing a shirt, the jacket/trouser combination looks much better won with something softer, such as a crepe or satin blouse.
- It is quite usual to dress up a jacket and trousers for an after-office event with jewellery and a change of shoes, but please don't make the mistake of changing flat work shoes for shoes with heels; the trousers will be too short – a change of heel heights needs a change of trousers.

High waisted

'I know I'm never going to be Kate Moss or Jean Shrimpton, so I have found what I hope is a form of dressing that pays some heed to current fashion and makes me feel as good as possible. Certain things are disallowed after a certain age including skirts above the knee and dresses without sleeves!' — Diana Donovan

'Dress for yourself – and don't listen to what other people say you should be wearing.' — Dame Judi Dench

# Borrowing from a Man's Wardrobe

Some of the most attractive and well-dressed women I know wear mainly men's clothes, right down to the shoes. It's a good look and a good idea and I do it all the time – not at all to achieve a totally masculine look but rather the opposite – the right pieces borrowed from a male wardrobe can complement your other clothes and can indeed emphasize your femininity.

*Men's shirt*

### Shirts

A man's shirt is the first covetable wardrobe item to wear both at the weekend, on holiday and to sleep in , so 'borrow' older shirts, particularly if they are linen.

Good shirts may be worn over jeans and trousers of any sort. Roll the cuffs back and wear a camisole or T-shirt in case they gape. If you are slim you can belt the shirt if you want, but for larger silhouettes, I think loose looks best.

### Trousers

I like the slightly forgiving cut of men's tailoring, but unless you are the same height and size as your man, you may find that borrowing trousers is not an option. But shopping in men's departments for jeans, chinos or cords is not a bad idea at all.

Bomber jacket

# 'Women often look wonderful in men's hats; look for them in vintage and charity shops. And try specialist fishing shops; they often have really good outdoor hats...'

### Jackets

The trouser rule also applies to borrowing jackets, although an oversized jacket can look good when worn informally. Also men's jackets tend to be straight, and I prefer gently shaped jackets with a slightly defined waist.

Borrowed bomber jackets, currently fashionable, are forgiving in shape and – if you like them, can work with jeans, as they are basically sexless in style.

### Hats

The same thing applies to men's hats, in which women often look wonderful. Look for them in vintage and charity shops. And try specialist fishing shops too; they often have really good outdoor hats.

To avoid looking butch in men's cast-offs, when wearing the trousers and jackets either add a beautiful blouse, perhaps lace-trimmed or in a soft silk or chiffon, or a colourful scarf or shawl, to soften the look.

### Shoes

Most men these days wear pretty awful shoes which most fastidious women would not want to be seen dead in under any circumstances, but interestingly some beautiful old shoes like brogues, loafers and other classic styles (which, strangely, tend to be smaller in size than modern men's shoes) and which can look equally good on women can be found in vintage and charity shops (as, sometimes, can old, smaller jackets). It's a good look that works well for winter in the country and at other time with casual trousers and jeans.

*Lace-up classic*

# And Other Options...

### Vintage

Vintage shops are fashionable in themselves now and much is made in the fashion press of scouring charity shops and speciality shops for vintage women's clothes. I think that these pieces are absolutely great for the young – vintage floral dresses with biker boots, for example – but on the whole if I were to wear 1950s clothes, unsurprisingly I would just look like my mother.

An exception can sometimes be made for certain couture or semi-couture pieces such as old Valentino or St Laurent – but they are expensive and hard to find.

### Second Hand

I did find some very good cashmere jumpers recently in a charity shop, but in general you have to be discerning – more so than with brand-new clothes – so generally I would recommend avoiding second-hand clothes, unless the owner is known to be very good at editing the selection and you have a very clear idea of what you are looking for.

### Ethnic

I'm a big fan of ethnic, or boho style. I love gypsy skirts and colourful Indian prints. But be careful not to look as though you've been in the dressing-up box. This is a look for summer not winter. High summer and holidays is a time to break out and wear fun items such as florals, long skirts, wide floppy trousers, sandals with pedicured and painted toes, of course, as well as glamorous colours, which look great in bright sunlight. It's a very liberating time fashion wise. I find it tempting to overdo it and sometimes feel I have taken the gypsy theme too far. Knowing when and where to stop is difficult, but on the terrace in warm glorious weather I tend to feel it really doesn't matter too much.

'Nothing beats those unlooked-for discoveries in charity shops or high street chains that you can mix with something special and dish up with your own personal twist. That's just good fun.'

— Dame Harriet Walter

# Hitting the Shops

Some people say they hate shopping but, really, it can be fun; like the best campaigns, military and otherwise, you should identify what you need and make a plan. It's a fact that it takes a long time to shop, and you really do need to allow yourself the time if you're going to be successful, although you don't of course have to do it all in one day.

It can be a good idea to take someone with you when you go shopping. Many people think they should shop with a friend, but a friend, really? Will she be honest? In truth, most friends do not want you to look better than them. A daughter is often a better choice as she does not want you to look stupid and embarrass her. And if daughters are not in the equation then consider a surrogate daughter – someone from a different generation, someone you like and whose style you appreciate and who will be honest with you. They will be flattered to be asked!

The alternative is, of course, to shop online. This takes away a lot of the pain, but many are not yet versed in the mechanics of this challenge and it does take a bit of getting used to, so perhaps practise with buying something simple or inexpensive first before you embark on looking for an entire wardrobe.

## Designer Brands

The best fashion magazines show us wonderful designer styles each season and often one is tempted to search out a particular brand, but it is an expensive occupation. If you do shop regularly for the big brands, both international and British, then I very much support you – wonderful on-trend shapes and fabrics, inspiration and quality come from the international catwalk shows and there is no need to not go to these departments and shops if you have something important to attend. The same applies to shoes - there is nothing like a pair of Manolos to perk you, or your outfit, up.

These brands may have sales worth going to so keep an eye out for announcements. The big discount warehouses may also be worth visiting. Remember that you will be buying old season's merchandise, although that need not matter, particularly for more classic items.

# What to Buy on the High Street

Mass-market retail style, the preserve of the chain stores, or what we call high street fashion in the UK, is irresistible and brilliant these days – I'm always in and out of Top Shop, H&M, Zara and Cos. Since cheap lighter fabrics usually look better than cheap heavier-weight material, it follows that chain stores, on both sides of the Atlantic, are much better in summer than winter. Look, for example, for floppy palazzo pants in dark prints and silky fabrics that you can wear with a plain T-shirt.

- Casual cotton shirts can be good – but don't go for the very cheapest, as they are just too thin. Cheaper clothes are made with the minimum of necessary cloth so again try and buy one that is at least one size larger so that it doesn't pull under the arms or gape across the chest.
- I have bought some very good coats on the high street, it's true; but not cheap, cheap, rather from the top end – what you might call Top High Street. But even here, make sure that the cloth is of a certain quality otherwise it could look terrible from the first wear. And always allow that you may need to change the buttons to raise the coat to a higher level of sartorial gold.

'Accentuate the positive, delete the negative.' — Donna Karan

✓ Flattering

# What NOT to buy on the High Street

I would never buy smart trousers or a white silk shirt or a tuxedo jacket. The other day, thinking I was being so clever, I bought a synthetic shirt that looked very like silk; it was floppy and seemed to hang quite well. Mistake. It crumples, and is too see-through, and doesn't fool anyone. The moral: cheap see-through shirts are not a good look. I have been searching on the internet for a thick white shirt – not in cotton, but in crepe or silk of some sort – but so many are transparent and that's not what I want – I don't want to see straps and bits. Of course, if it's deliberately designed to be transparent then you must find a camisole to go under it.

Cheap trousers, unless they're summer holiday trousers like palazzo pants or printed trousers – see previous page – are also a mistake. They look wonderful in the shop and then you sit down and in no time at all they crease behind the knees and across the hips. Trousers are definitely something that are worth spending money on in my opinion.

'Crease-free clothes
are stress-free clothes
– which is why my
investment in Pleats
Please from Issey
Miyake, often over a
decade ago, prove that
I am as adroit with my
money as any hedge
fund manager.' — Suzy Menkes

 Too tight

# Shopping in the Sales

These days I do more sale shopping online than actually going to shops, but that is because I do know what I want – that route is reserved for a confident dresser. Most people will still go to shops for sale bargains, but a word of caution is needed – you can make a lot of mistakes in sales and your right to return items – never mind, get your money back (many stores tend to offer you only a credit note in the sale) – is often far more restricted than if you pay full price. Unless the item is faulty you are unlikely to be able to return it just because you have changed your mind, so always check with each store's policy before you splash the cash.

'Don't forget that in a sale, fashion – as opposed to stylish – items are, by definition, no longer fashion; they're there because it's the end of the season, and the shop needs to refresh its stock.'

Perversely, my biggest sales regrets are when I DON'T buy something in a sale – only recently I saw an expensive, beautifully made coat in a sale and I went away without buying it, went back later and of course it had been sold. So I try to make that particular mistake less and less now – if it's a very good quality garment that you have spotted, even if it costs a bit more, you won't regret it. So I think you should use sales to buy good things – a well-cut jacket, trousers that fit, good cashmere.

But don't forget that fashion – as opposed to stylish – items in a sale are, by definition, no longer fashion; they're in the sale because it's the end of the season and the shop needs to refresh its stock with new items, so they're dated before you even wear them. Of course, that only matters if you live among fashionistas and since most people don't, then it really doesn't matter as long as you like the piece and it suits you.

That said, I am quite a conservative character, and I do think that I, and many others like me, would do well to have a bit more what-the-hell in our fashion lives. So when, in the sales, you see a wonderful beaded, printed and colourful top that you love, just buy it, and have some fun...

'My personal rule book is as follows:

1. Accept what you cannot wear at this age, and eliminate those styles and colours from your dress code.

2. Decide what you need, not what you like but cannot use.

3. Decide whether an outfit is one that can be worn often or a one-off show stopper. And if it is the latter, better to forget it because you will regret its expense and lack of occasions to wear it – or worse, know that it has been seen and will be remembered.'

— HRH Princess Michael of Kent

# Internet Shopping

Online shopping is great fun – really. First, there is the enormous pleasure or not having to venture out and trek around the shops yourself. Secondly, it is easy enough to engage in and as it is global, and relatively sophisticated in its mechanics, you can buy from suppliers, shops and makers large and small. And, best of all, of course, you can try on items in the comfort and privacy of your own home, in your own time. You can see how something looks with your other clothes, and can also try it on with the right underwear and foot wear so that you can properly assess how it looks.

'Many websites now are more like magazines than shopping sites, with short features on new styles and the clothes broken down on the site into useful, separate departments.'

There are a lot of extremely good shopping sites out there, where you can find very nice, and often unusual, clothes. And not just from local shops. The internet gives you instant access to a huge range of clothes – from large companies to individual designers – something that is particularly useful if you don't live near a large city or if your local shopping options are particularly poor.

The sites have moved onwards – and upwards – since the first early pioneering ones. The best are chatty, helpful and very user-friendly; many of them being more like magazines than websites, with short features on new styles and the clothes for sale broken down on the site into separate 'departments', ranging from trouser types to sections that are filled with ideas for specific occasions such as weddings and other formal events. They allow you to amble from the sofa to the rail or to window-shop from a comfortable chair.

All internet companies are becoming much better at getting your new buy to you as quickly and easily as possible – and there are collection sites springing up (see below) for those who don't want their buys delivered to their home.

Internet shopping sites have also improved hugely in helping you to return your new buy if you don't want it once you've seen it. The best sites offer a variety of options to help you return things and don't forget – they EXPECT you to reject and return stuff, just as you might in a store changing room. But again, check the policy of each particular site before you blithely order 20 different items.

'Once you've measured yourself accurately, write down your measurements and keep them close by so that you always have access to them and don't have to keeep bringing out the tape measure.'

And of course, internet shopping is not just limited to shops and manufacturers based in your own country. Global delivery options are growing and becoming easier to access all the time (I once bought a very pretty swimsuit from a company based in the US Virgin Islands).

### Finding your Right Size

- First of all, since you are not going to be able to try anything on before you buy it, finding your right size – which may of course vary according from manufacturer to manufacturer – is vital.
- This is not a moment for cheating – you should measure yourself accurately; luckily, most shopping websites have measurement guides to help you check what size you will need.
- When you've faced the measured truth, write down your measurements, and keep them close by so that you have always access them – and don't have to keep bringing out the tape measure.

### Returning Stuff

Many people are put off the idea of internet shopping because of the perceived difficulty of returning anything you don't like. But the whole process has become so much easier now. Obviously it is most important to check both the medium and the small print to see the seller's terms – particularly to see whether the customer or the supplier pays if you want to return items. Distance selling offers extra protection in that, within a limited time – usually seven days – you have time to examine the item before deciding whether to keep it or not. Some sites offer free returns as a matter of course, but for those that don't, look out for periods when they are offering special offers on free delivery/returns. This is a good time to try out a site you haven't used before.

If you're not sure of the size, order more then one of the same item in different sizes to try. As I wrote earlier, within this new shopping arena, online companies actively expect you to return items – up to 40 per cent of clothing bought online is returned, with the percentages even higher for closely fitting items such as dresses. Some companies have a return code (indicating why you are sending it back) for 'multiple size order' that covers exactly this situation. Be cautious though – with the rise and rise of internet sales, some online retailers are now looking at the process of returning clothes, in terms of quantities and so forth, so again, check before you order.

———

Think you will be out when the parcel arrives? You can have parcels delivered to your work address, or many companies now have arrangements for centralized drop off /collection points in convenience stores or at railway stations. Click-and Collect is also gaining in popularity as a sort of half-way house between internet and store shopping where you order online from a store and designate a convenient branch from which to collect your order.

———

Wise words from
Well-dressed Women...

'Don't move out of your
comfort zone and experiment
too much. I am against
experimentation – stay with
your own life-long style and
keep it simple.' — Grace Coddington

'Know yourself and be
comfortable with that
knowledge.' — Joan Burstein

'Perhaps because I dress up for a living, I usually choose clothes that won't attract too much attention but which make me feel good when I have to scrub up nice for some special occasion. I have stayed roughly the same size for the last 30 years and I love recycling some old favourite I had forgotten I owned, and pairing it with something I bought last week.' — Dame Harriet Walter

# When to Wear

My hope is that now you have read the earlier sections of this book you now feel happy with the everyday needs of dressing to suit yourself, and feel comfortable with yourself and what you are wearing – which is the most important thing. It's time therefore to think about dressing for your everyday social life – including not just the grander events, which we tackle, but also the more everyday challenges – the occasional lunch, interview or meeting that demand a certain amount of thought.

Remember that life, on many levels, is much less formal today, and looking good no longer means dressing extremely formally. You will be more relaxed if you are comfortable in what you are wearing, so choose a well-fitting skirt or pair of trousers, worn with a simple coat or jacket. Forget wearing high heels unless you do so on a daily basis – go for something lower, or flat shoes which can now be very fashionable. Don't force yourself into anything you are uncertain about.

# Going Out

Just as what you wear in the day is less formal than it used to be, so too is the way we dress in the evening for what one might call the simpler side of social life – all the more informal ways of spending pleasant time. Again, as with dressing in the day, it is important to feel relaxed about what you are wearing but it is also fun to dress up a bit – after all when are you going to, if not now? I tend to have one or two tried and tested pieces, or outfits, each season, which I know will work without too much thought on my part and which – sometimes with a bit or tweaking – will fit almost any bill.

'Another good shape that you can just slip on and go is the shift, useful for those of us who have lost most semblance of a waist and whose tummy now veers towards the convex...'

A well-cut, knee-length, pencil skirt in a lighter fabric – not a tweed or heavy wool, but a gabardine, crepe or figured fabric – is one such staple that I wear either with a cashmere or silk jumper or a tunic top. My second staple is a well-cut, non-saggy or unintentionally baggy, pair of trousers, again made in a slightly lighter fabric than that which I might wear in the day, with a choice of tops that I have already tried and tested. And, depending on the occasion, a jacket that complements the shape of the trousers – in fact, a well cut trouser-suit or a tuxedo suit. I also try – as we have talked about earlier in the book – to have at least one dress that I can just slip on and go – in my case usually a wrap, knee-length design. Another really useful shape is the shift, for those of us who have lost any semblance of a waist and whose tummy veers towards the convex.

I also make sure that I have the right pair – or pairs – of shoes for all three options as I find that trying on shoes to go with a particular outfit, looking at heel heights and so on, can take longer than choosing what to wear in the first place. I finish with a bit of jewellery – particularly something round the neck, and I'm ready to go.

Pencil skirt

# Dressing Up

Next we come to what to wear for special occasions. Throughout my career I have been asked questions about what to wear in specific circumstances. It's not, of course easy to answer in a few words as it means categorizing such events – weddings in particular – into a narrow box. For all such occasion dressing, the cardinal rule is to avoid feeling that you should change the essential idea of what you have worked out that suits you, just because it is a special occasion. Stick to the basic rules that you have set yourself, such as the right shape and length for you and then ratchet up the thinking on colour and texture.

**Outdoor Evenings**

I have noticed a sort of uniform at this type of occasion and I don't always like what I see. Pretty women bring out the same jackets, skirts and shawls every year, and it shows. It is not just that the garment is out-of-date, it's also that old things suffer wear and tear and just because you only wear it two or three times a year doesn't mean that it still looks as good as new. It doesn't – and, believe me, it doesn't look charmingly 'vintage' either. An old velvet jacket will wear at the cuffs, shine at the elbows, and the pile will flatten where it was once caught in a rain shower; the long printed skirt and blouse will look floppy instead of crisp, and the trousers will be sagging and bagging in the wrong places.

Treat yourself to something new – regardless of how much you want to spend, do try and freshen up that once-a-year outfit from time to time. You will feel so much better and have more fun – even if you are one of those women who hate dressing up.

Summer al fresco formal evening events such as garden operas are delightful. With luck the weather will be warm-ish and the whole evening a lovely experience. However longish al fresco evenings do set their own – often physical – challenges so here's a thought – rather than start with your dress, instead start with your shoes, as what you wear on your feet when you are outside is really important.

'Every woman should be an edition de luxe of herself.'

— Sydney Tremain

You may be tempted to wear any old, comfortable, shoes because you think they won't be seen. Trust me, they will; and once they are noticed, they will destroy the rest of the image that you have so carefully put together. Flat shoes – new ( there is no excuse not to buy some for the occasion as they don't have to be expensive and can be discarded if they are ruined by the terrain and the weather) and relatively light will be fine – much better that than a pair of loafers. And if flat shoes don't work with the dress or trouser shape you have chosen, then a wedge heel is a good alternative and again can be bought relatively cheaply and in a variety of heights.

And if you will be expected to sit on the ground – for a picnic perhaps – whether you are wearing wedge shoes or flat, a long skirt or trousers make life a lot more comfortable, coupled with a shawl or pretty jacket, which is a useful and elegant addition.

Many Indian shops (try Maharani in London) have a good choice of cotton or silk jackets in plain colours or simple prints. If you prefer something more structured, then look for a tuxedo jacket – which is a long, tailored jacket, the proportions of which look best with trousers or long skirts – or perhaps a shorter, tailored one, in a gabardine weight, or even velvet, although the latter is not a great choice if you think you are likely to be rained on. A shorter jacket, depending on your figure, works best with soft, mid-length skirt, or wide-legged soft or silk trousers.

Long dresses look very pretty at outdoor summer events and softer skirts are more comfortable when sitting down for long periods or for candle-lit outdoor picnics, and they have the added advantage of not creasing as obviously as a straight skirt will. A beaded cardigan or jacket with a long, pretty dress looks less bulky than a tailored jacket – as does a glamorous long shawl.

# And another thing...

These days I am aware of my slightly Michelin-esque midriff and so like rather high or slightly raised waistlines. It is a flattering look for the evening, when you don't want to be corseted, although I do feel that corseting beneath an evening dress can be a good thing – making you feel and look slimmer, and therefore more confident. Beware the bulges though, with anything too tight (see Back to Basics pages 20–23 on underwear for more on this).

'Evening dresses
that suit me in
colour and style
I often "retire"
into my wardrobe,
and resurrect
some years later,
perhaps with a
small addition – a
flower, an organza
shawl.' — HRH Princess Michael of Kent

'A long dress that doesn't quite reach the floor is a mistake, so choose shoes with a heel height that ensures that the hem just skims the ground.'

## Black Tie Glamour

Men are lucky here as black tie, for them, means what it says; nothing much can go wrong – although I have seen more than a few catastrophes over the years, but that's another book...

For women, black tie on an invitation these days can mean anything from a little black dress to a full-blown ball gown, and it is not always easy to know which direction to take.

If in doubt call up the hostess or organizer if it is a charity event and check. Arriving in a short little black dress when all around you are wearing long can send the most confident or fashion-aware guest into a spin. Should the worst happen then confidence will have to carry you through; remember what Oscar Wilde said – it is you who have been invited , not your clothes, or words to that effect.

A good 'black-tie' long dress should make you feel at your confident best: it should fit well, have a flattering neckline, long-ish sleeves and fall to the ground (unless it is deliberately designed to end at mid-calf). A long dress that doesn't quite reach the floor is a mistake, so choose shoes with a heel height that ensure that the hem just skims the ground. Deep, rich-coloured prints and luscious fabrics can be lovely, particularly in winter. Personally, I find that bright summer prints are too easily recognized on the dress's subsequent outings, so I try and avoid anything but the subtlest prints in summer, unless the dress is cheap and therefore relatively dispensable. And finally, if in doubt, always dress up rather than down – your hostess will be flattered and you will look great.

Formal events often mean a fair amount of standing about, and if there is dancing your feet come under even more pressure, so I like to choose comfortable shoes. I know that they are not easy to find – the shops are full of high heels, when all you want is an elegant court shoe on a medium or low heel. Persevere in the search – flat shoes are tempting and may work in a practical sense but you need to be elegant on a formal occasion or you will feel dumpy. I promise that you will probably feel better if you are wearing some sort of heel; it will give you confidence – and improve your deportment.

**Party Points**
- If possible buy something new each year – a shirt, trousers, shoes perhaps.
- New fabrics mean that a long dress in certain fine cottons or manmade fibres will not crease, will let you breathe and keep its shape the whole evening.
- Look for a dress with sleeves, but if you prefer sleeveless think about a jacket to wear with it, as a cardigan (unless it is an embellished evening one) obviously doesn't look quite right at a formal evening event. A plain colour is often smarter and more striking than a print.
- A hooded jacket with a deep hood (and I dont mean an anorak) can be useful if the evening is wet – beats carrying an umbrella around.
- I always take a scarf or a wrap as well; if the evening is damp it keeps your hair in place.

# Weddings

One of the most challenging of dress conundrums, no matter what your age, is what to wear at a wedding – whether as a guest, the mother of the bride or indeed the mother of the groom.

*Edge to edge*

'You don't need to have everything matching – in fact it is preferable if you do not – a matchy-matchy outfit looks as if you have been trying too hard.'

The first thing to say is that you don't necessarily have to buy an entirely new wedding wardrobe; often an outfit can be recycled, perhaps with a new hat or shoes. And remember that it is not necessary that everything matches – in fact it is actually preferable if they do not – a matchy-matchy outfit looks as if you have been trying too hard, rather than confidently knowing what to wear. The important thing is that you feel comfortable and good in what you wear.

- A dress worn with a coat or jacket is the favourite outfit for a wedding, particularly as a dress can be worn on its own if there is a dinner or dance to follow.
- I have seen very elegant women in immaculate wide trousers with long, unlined jackets at summer weddings, but unless you feel comfortable wearing unstructured clothes, I advise you not to try this look, as it is a style that can easily look under-dressed.
- If it is a country wedding, take a pair of flat or low-heeled shoes with you in case there are muddy fields to negotiate – there invariably are. I find wedge shoes good for summer weddings where lawns seem a regular challenge.
- And on your legs, flesh-coloured tights for winter legs exposed in summer are a must in my view; sun-kissed, naked legs are fine for the young, but very seldom does an elegant woman look good with bare legs at a formal occasion.

### Hats

Personally I am not a hat wearer although I love them on others; I have a big head and therefore buying off-the-peg is difficult as nothing fits – and too small a hat will give you a headache, that I guarantee. Even hiring a hat seems a good idea to me, but it is expensive. In desperation, I have resorted to Alice bands and attached a feather or flower, but I don't recommend this route unless it is something you have a natural talent for. Saying that, I did actually do that myself at my daughter's wedding and felt perfectly comfortable, particularly as the groom's mother did the same – and that was without any conferring!

If your head is a standard size, department stores these days have a very good selection, far better than in the past, as do many vintage shops. If at all possible try any hat on with your outfit, or at the very least with the jacket – before you buy – so that you can look at the broader, overall picture. And as always, try and look at yourself in a full-length mirror rather than one that shows only your head.

Covered

Ribbon

'I am eager
to bring back
cocktail hats -
small, chic and
serving as a frame
to a picture.'

— HRH Princess Michael of Kent

If you do buy something new
then I recommend that you
wear it about the house a few
times before the day itself,
together with the shoes, hat
etc. It might surprise the odd
unexpected visitor or the
postman, but you will feel far
more comfortable and relaxed
in the whole outfit if you do.

Feathers.

# Holidays and Travel

Oh, thank heavens for holidays; you can wear almost anything you enjoy and not worry too much about the aesthetics – unless of course you are going on holiday with friends. In this scenario I would always ask my travelling companions what they are planning on packing; I might even ask someone who had been on a similar excursion what they took and what worked.

I travel a lot and packing is still a challenge. If you are going on a budget airline for a short break or for work, definitely buy a carry-on regulation size bag and keep it with you as otherwise it may well not arrive at your destination at the same time as you.

If you want to take a larger case, of course do so, but try not to buy one that is too large as, even with wheels, they are exhausting to manoeuvre and occasionally lift. The ideal, of course, is to pack only enough for the length of your stay – and not come back with a pile of things you didn't wear. I actually make a day-to-day list for the time I am away, and then count out the day and evening essentials for that period (with a couple of spare bits for the inevitable unexpected events) I know it is a bit OCD, but it works for me!

### Overnight trips

On a short working trip, in a good carry-on
bag, I would take a spongebag filled with
travel sample sizes (Muji do clear plastic bags
with zips which are very useful). I would wear
trousers or a skirt , a tunic top and the shoes
that will work the next day. Packed would
be a night-shirt, a skirt, a cashmere top and
a change of underwear. There would be a
pair of opaque and a pair of flesh-coloured
tights so that I could decide which to go for
depending on the weather. I might add a little
black uncrushable dress.

Were it a weekend trip I would base my
wardrobe round trousers – travelling in one
pair, packing another, with a couple of T-shirts,
a shirt or great top, a cardigan, a sweater in
winter, a lightweight raincoat and two pairs
of shoes – one for travelling and walking, one
for the evenings. Wearing a skirt to travel
does make some functions more efficient –
having to drop trousers onto the sometimes
unavoidable wet floor is then avoided...

'Tailoring is the unbeatable camouflage of the imperfect body. Look at all those ageing peacock males! Think about a bespoke jacket. Many tailors, defined as menswear creators, measure up and make for women too. The ultimate idea: a trip to Savile Row. Or to Naples!' — Suzy Menkes

'Always take a last look in the bathroom mirror to make sure you like what you see.' — Joan Burstein

### Only On the Beach

There are some things, that although you should avoid wearing at other times, can still look good on the beach. I think in the high summer with brown legs, you can get away with shorter skirts for instance – certainly for lounging around in the sun, by the pool, etc. Equally you can, under the same circumstances, choose to wear no sleeves. Because you feel better and you've taken a bit of colour many things that don't work at home look fine. Remember though – be careful and check the mirror even on holiday. And don't sit down to a meal in nothing but a swimsuit; not only is it probably inappropriate, but it is a time when the cameras may come out. Unfortunately, as you get older, to be immortalized sitting up in just a swimsuit can be, for many, an unflattering look. So since you still want to look your best, a thin cover-up is a good plan. For the photo opportunities wear your sunglasses – you will look younger.

### Ethnic

Some of those unusually shaped and very comfortable trousers are fine on the beach, and bold ethnic patterns also look good on holiday (almost the only place they do look good). Kurtas – the long shaped tunic shirts worn in India – are great in summer; they can look good with trousers at a summer lunch, pressed, starched and worn with gold earrings – a good look with white trousers, or wide linen trousers in a complementary colour. African kaftans are a wonderful cover up and hide many evils and are perfect for weekends and holidays. Cotton jersey is the most amenable of fabrics to pack and works well in hot weather. Better high street shops usually carry both dresses and skirts as well as trousers in cotton jersey and are well worth searching out.

*Indian chapel sandal*

### Shoes

It is a temptation to take far too many shoes
on holiday, whether it is on a sight-seeing trip
or a more leisurely break. Shoes add weight
and take up space and you won't wear them all.
Be ruthless.

A pair of silver or gold sandals that will work
in the evening as well as during the day; a
pair of tan flat shoes or sandals and a pair of
plimsolls or light sneakers; these should see
you through almost every contingency and go
with everything in your holiday wardrobe.

**Buying a Swimsuit – Facing the Truth**
It might seem obvious, but it is well worth
going somewhere good and buying a
properly constructed swimsuit. I do
have one, because it's nice to have one
gorgeous swimsuit, but they can be very
expensive indeed.

You can of course buy on the high street. I bought
two very pretty swimsuits there this year – both
one-pieces, properly boned round the bosom and
with a bit of gathering around the tummy. And –
which I think is important – just like with cheap
dresses, I bought them a size bigger so they didn't
cut in and cut up under your bottom and into
your back. They came with adjustable, removable
straps – particularly important since if you've got a
big bosom, you need straps.

As far as colour goes, plain, bright colours look
wonderful in the sun – but I do think you've
got to be careful with patterns. I'm just not
sure that bright, light prints work, but in the
end if it's a print you really love, then why not –
particularly if you are buying more than one.

Always machine wash
your swimsuit when you
get home on a cool wash
because you've got to get
the chlorine and the salt
out – this is imperative.

'Decide what to wear from your wardrobe and what to continue wearing.'

— Grace Coddington

'I believe passionately that my clothes should work as hard as I do – and that applies to someone still jetting around the world or who prefers playing tennis to doing the ironing.'

— Suzy Menkes

# Wise words from Well-dressed Women...

'There are some fabulous older women dressers out there who don't tend to care any more what other people think of them. They dress for themselves and express their personality through their clothes. To some, clothes are pure adornment, almost an art form. They bedeck themselves with wonderful coloured fabrics and eccentric jewels. Although it is not for me, I love that.'

— Dame Harriet Walter

'Feel confident with yourself and everything will fit you.' — Farida Khelfa

'Remember to try and let go of the image you had when you were younger and be happy ageing gracefully.' — Joan Burstein

# P.S... After Cancer

While putting this book together I received a body blow in the form of cancer. I had to stop everything for a period in order to recover. During that time I had a lot of time for reflection and as I result I am adding this chapter for those who may have been in a similar position. This is purely from an appearance point of view of course. I leave everything else to the experts.

The first thing I needed to address was a very sore stomach where I had been operated on. Even the soft *elastic* of pyjamas caused discomfort, so I switched to nighties. A nice old fashioned nightie is a very comforting garment.

During the day I had the same problem: my waist. Jerry Hall has said never wear elasticated trousers because you can't tell when you are putting on weight. She is right: a good observation. For me though, they were the only answer and I even resorted to jogging pants when at home.

When I went out I did smarten up a bit, as much for my own morale as for those I was meeting. I found body-con dresses out of the question, as my pot-belly meant that I just was not the right shape anymore. I looked for endless tunic shapes and wore short ones over narrow or wide elasticated trousers and longer skirts. I took a fall shortly after the operation and after that never wore anything but flat shoes.

Even in flat shoes I am still frightened of falling and with good reason. I fell again on some stairs and received many bruises, and I was wearing thick soled flat 'slides'. I think it must be a balance problem and one has to be very careful. No leather-soled shoes at all as you can go flying in wet weather, particularly on glass pavement lights. If you do buy a shoe with a leather sole take it straight to the heel bar and get them to add a non-slip rubber sole.

For the evening I venture out in kitten heels but I take them in a bag and put them on when I arrive wherever I am going. Sadly for me it seems that my days in higher heels are over. Less elegant perhaps but I am secretly relieved.

The biggest challenge of all was the loss of hair. Early on I had my head shaved as the hair began falling in great clumps. I then experimented with various forms of headgear.

A friend brought me a selection of berets in many colours from Paris and I wore them constantly. They are a bit unforgiving when there is no hair to soften the look, but they sit firmly in place in all weathers and are very easy to put on. This is more than can be said for scarves. Tying a scarf into an attractive shape is not easy and a lot of mirror-practice took place. Some moments of extreme frustration, too. You can find turban-like head wear online for exactly this problem and I did buy one, but in the main I relied on various scarves in many colours. Slippery fabrics do not work well, as everything constantly becomes un-tied. Choose a scarf with some texture; wool or cotton muslin-type weaves are best. Fold the scarf diagonally to get the best flexibility as you tie it. For the evening I found a black taffeta scarf which tied brilliantly and looked quite glamorous. I might add a brooch to the scarf and almost always added earrings to brighten things up.

Make-up too was a challenge. When you lose your hair your eyebrows and lashes go too, leaving a pale piggy-eyed patient. I went shopping with my daughter for eyeliner, mascara and eyebrow pencils. I chose soft brown and grey rather than black, so the contrast wasn't too strong. Again, having not worn anything but mascara for years, applying these new products was challenging, and I spent many moments in front of a magnifying mirror each time I went out. The process was not helped by the fact that I need glasses and trying to apply eye make-up behind them is a challenge in itself. Carine Roitfeld, the French style icon, has been quoted as saying that smudged eyed make-up is very sexy; just as well in my case (although I never felt remotely sexy).

It is important in this sort of situation to try and hang on to one's sense of humour, otherwise it could be tears of frustration all the way. Try and detach yourself from the whole thing and see yourself as a character in a comedy act if you can.

Share your experiences with a friend who has been or is in a similar position. It is so refreshing not having to try and say the right things and not embarrass other people. Being irreverent with someone who understands is a great relief and a good laugh is good for you, and for them.

As a treat I was taken by a friend to a nail bar and treated to a manicure. It was a really good, kind thing to do. My friend came too and also had her nails done. Perfect opportunity for a good gossip, and you leave feeling pampered and relaxed.

Remember, friends want to be there for you and want you to let them spoil you; it really is hugely life-enhancing. Don't feel shy about approaching them.

Good friends will always understand when they are not needed but will be there for you when you want them.

# Credits and Acknowledgements

I would like to thank the following of all shapes and sizes for their unfailing encouragement, inspiration and support.

Caroline Clifton-Mogg, Meredith Etherington-Smith, Sian Parkhouse, Helen McFarland, Alfonso Iacurci, Jonathan Harvey, Karina Dobrotvorskaya, Fiona Steel, Stephanie Halfmann, Natalie Theo, Camilla Morton, Juliet Hughes-Hallett, Clare Casey, Lucy Snowdon, Kimberly Quinn, Harriet Wilson, Annie Holcroft, Frances Bentley. Vanessa de Lisle, Emma Goad, Hatti Cossart, Davina Alexander, Gina Price, Jo Allison, Charlotte Scott, Fiona Hayes, Sally Blundell, Prue Dawson, Sarah Caldecott, Willie Christie, Lucinda Chambers, Elizabeth Fallon, Maureen Gerber, Pat Pichler, Clarissa de Pass. Camilla Lowther, Sophie Hicks, Tessa Balfour. Isabel Cazalet, Nonie Ward, Colette Douglas-Home, Felicity Clark, Sarah Cunningham-Reid, Penelope Phillips, Jane Taylor,  Jo Allison, Sarah Manley, Vicki Sarge, Diana Donovan, Bunty Lewis, Robin Muir, Frances Heaton, Sarah Mahaffy, Harriet Wilson

and all my beloved family

and those wonderful friends and colleagues who agreed to give me invaluable quotes for this little book.

# Internet Suppliers

**Farfetch**
www.farfetch.com/uk

**Net-a- porter**
www.net-a-porter.com

**The Outnet**
www.theoutnet.com

**Matches**
www.matchesfashion.com/
womens

**Mytheresa**
www.mytheresa.com/en-gb

**Coggles**
www.coggles.com/home.dept

**Browns**
www.brownsfashion.com

**Harvey Nichols**
www.harveynichols.com

**Selfridges**
www.selfridges.com

**Style**
www.style.com

**Norstrom US**
www.nordstromrack.com

**House of Fraser**
www.houseoffraser.com

**Marina Rinaldi**
www.marinarinaldi.com
Very good for larger figures

**Liberty**
www.liberty.co.uk

**Harrods**
www.harrods.com

**Boutique1**
www.boutique1.com

**Winser**
www.winserlondon.com

**John Lewis**
www.johnlewis.com

**Donnaida**
www.donnaida.com
Excellent site for jeans

**Vestiaire Collective**
www.vestiairecollective.com
Vestaire Collective has been
creeping up on the internet
radar. An upmarket cross
between an outlet and a
purveyor of smart vintage
clothes, they stock pre-worn
designs from designers like
Chanel and Isabel Marant and
others, as well as older pieces
and end-of-range.

**Dressipi**
www.dressipi.com
Dressipi is a personalized
styling and shopping service